Working with Manuscripts

Working with Manuscripts

A Guide for Textual Scholars

LIV INGEBORG LIED

AND

BRENT NONGBRI

Yale UNIVERSITY PRESS

New Haven and London

Published with assistance from the foundation established in memory of Calvin Chapin of the Class of 1788, Yale College.

Copyright © 2025 by Yale University.
All rights reserved.

This book may not be reproduced, in whole or in part, including illustrations, in any form (beyond that copying permitted by Sections 107 and 108 of the U.S. Copyright Law and except by reviewers for the public press), without written permission from the publishers.

Yale University Press books may be purchased in quantity for educational, business, or promotional use. For information, please e-mail sales.press@yale.edu (U.S. office) or sales@yaleup.co.uk (U.K. office).

Set in Minion type by Westchester Publishing Services.
Printed in the United States of America.

Library of Congress Control Number: 2024940730
ISBN 978-0-300-26442-5 (paperback)

A catalogue record for this book is available from the British Library.

10 9 8 7 6 5 4 3 2 1

Contents

Acknowledgments vii

Introduction 1

ONE. Manuscripts as Artifacts 9

TWO. Finding Your Manuscript 41

THREE. Provenance and Why It Matters 63

FOUR. Getting Access and Planning Your Stay 89

FIVE. In the Reading Room with Your Manuscript 108

SIX. Back Home—What Now? 136

SEVEN. Asking for Help 144

EIGHT. Publishing and Permissions 156

Conclusions 165

Glossary 167

Notes 175

Index 177

Acknowledgments

This is the book we wished we had when we started working with manuscripts. It is based on the experiences we have had (and mistakes we have made) over the course of many years of manuscript research. It may not answer all your questions, but we hope that it comes in handy as you enter the exciting world of manuscripts.

Each of us was responsible for drafting about half the text, and we have revised and reworked each other's writing throughout. We regard the result as a joint effort, and we would like to thank Mary Pasti for copyediting the whole. Thanks also to Jennifer Banks and the team at Yale University Press for seeing the project through to publication.

We are indebted to Garrick V. Allen, Jennifer W. Knust, AnneMarie Lujdendijk, Matthew P. Monger, Michael P. Penn, Michael Press, and Blossom Stefaniw for reading and responding to chapter drafts or larger parts of the book. We are also grateful to Årstein Justnes and the contributors to The Lying Pen of Scribes project for both inspiring and supporting the writing of this book. The production of the book also benefited from a second project, The Early History of the Codex (EthiCodex, 2021–2026). We thank the Research Council of

Norway for supporting both projects. Thanks also to the three anonymous readers who reviewed the manuscript for Yale University Press and provided very helpful feedback. Finally, thanks to Mary Jane Cuyler and Eystein Gullbekk for their encouragement and patience.

Working with Manuscripts

Introduction

Have you ever seen the manuscripts that carry the ancient texts you are studying? Have you ever seen any early manuscript at all? Do you wonder what it might be like to interact with an ancient, handwritten document, to examine how the text is laid out on the page, to see how it feels to leaf through a medieval book or unroll a scroll? Are you curious about engaging with actual material artifacts from the past but perhaps overwhelmed and even a bit anxious about entering unfamiliar territory? If so, you are not alone.

Although **manuscripts** are a rarity in most parts of the world today, they were once ubiquitous. Before the introduction of the printing press, literature was preserved and transmitted through the creation of handwritten **copies**. Each of the copies, being the work of one or more copyists, contains variant readings, mistakes, corrections, and many other unique features. The manuscripts that contain these copies are the sources of all textual scholarship. Scholars who study texts from antiquity and the Middle Ages, however, often use as their primary sources, not these artifacts themselves but **critical editions**. These editions have been prepared by experts who use the divergent manuscripts to produce a hybrid text that then serves as the basis for interpretation, with variant readings relegated to the **critical apparatus** at the bottom of the page. What is created in these critical editions is generally assumed to correspond to an early state of the text, or even to the actual words of the author. Because of traditional divisions in academic labor and the increasing demands of specialization, many **textual scholars**, people who have spent years or even decades gaining intimate knowledge of texts, have not been trained to work on manuscripts. They rely upon the critical editions, so the intriguing world of manuscripts often remains outside their field of view.

Critical editions, at their best, can be excellent tools for engaging with the manuscripts. There is no doubt that critical editions make life easier by giving a sensible rendering of ancient texts so that those of us who want to read the texts don't have to read every surviving manuscript. But what might we be missing by not getting to know the manuscripts that carry the texts? Take a look at Figure I.1.

This is a page from a manuscript containing the letters of the apostle Paul in Greek, the Codex Coislinianus (abbreviated as H or 015 in modern editions of the Greek New Testament), which was probably produced in the sixth century. In fact, it is the final **leaf** of this manuscript. But the text on this page is not from the letters of Paul. Instead, this last leaf contains a note from the **copyist**. It reads: "I wrote and edited this volume of Paul the Apostle, arranging it in lines to the best of my ability. . . . The book was collated against the copy of the library in Caesarea written by the hand of the holy Pamphilus." This note in the manuscript, though not part of the "text" of Paul's letters, still tells us something about the history of the text that matters for the interpretation of the text: If the note is accurate, this text was at some stage corrected against a copy

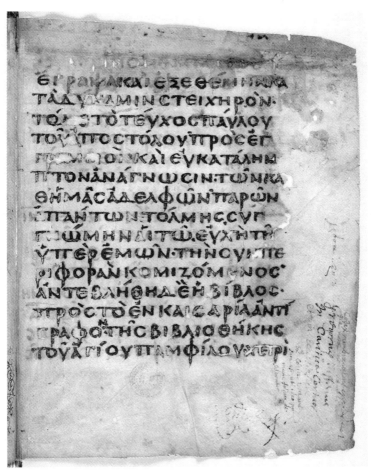

FIGURE I.1. The last leaf of a codex of Paul's letters in Greek (Codex Coislinianus), showing a note from the copyist: Paris, Bibliothèque nationale de France, Coislin 202, fol. 14 recto. (Image courtesy of the Bibliothèque nationale de France, Paris.)

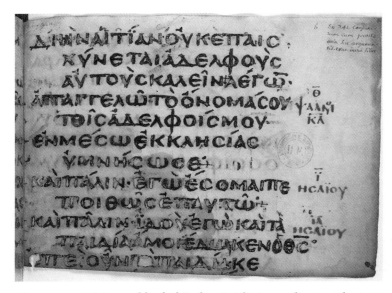

FIGURE I.2. A trimmed leaf of Codex Coislinianus showing the text of Hebrews 2:11–14 written in sense lines, with scriptural references added as marginal annotations: Paris, Bibliothèque nationale de France, Coislin 202, fol. 6 recto. (Image courtesy of the Bibliothèque nationale de France, Paris.)

produced by the famous scholar Pamphilus of Caesarea, who was active in the third century.

And if we look at another page from this manuscript, one that contains a portion of the letter to the Hebrews (2:11–14), we get a clearer idea of what the copyist means by the phrase "arranging it in lines" (Figure I.2).

The copyist has written the text in **sense lines**, a type of **sense unit** that uses spacing and **eisthesis** (indentation of lines) to create sections of differing length that correspond to a grammatical phrase. Notice how different the **layout** of this page is from the layout of the page in Figure I.1. This kind of division

Introduction 5

of the text is informative. It can provide insight into how the copyist of the manuscript, or the copyist of the **exemplar** that was used as a model, understood the text. It also shows us how ancient readers of the manuscript encountered the text. Also notice the writing in the **margins**, which points out the sources of the quotations in the text: Psalm 21 and the book of Isaiah.

If you look closely at the letters on these two pages, you might notice some other interesting features. Every letter has been carefully traced over in a darker ink, possibly suggesting that the manuscript was used for a long period of time and required new ink to remain legible. Accent marks have been added, perhaps indicating that this manuscript was read out loud at some point. The leaf in Figure I.2 has obviously been cut from what was once a larger leaf, but notice that in Figure I.1, some partial letters preserved at the top of the page show that this leaf was also trimmed down (in fact, all the surviving leaves of this manuscript are mutilated to some extent). The parchment of the manuscript shows various stains. The edges of both pages have additional writing in different Latin scripts written cursively. Both pages also have an impression from a circular owner's stamp. All of this is evidence of the later use of this manuscript at a time long after it was produced.

Looking at the manuscript itself thus sheds important light on the text of Paul's letters carried by the manuscript— namely, it is said to have been checked against a copy written by the noted scholar Pamphilus of Caesarea. It also provides insight into the life of the manuscript itself, from the time of its production through its use by later readers and its movement into a new (Latin) linguistic context.

The recognition that individual manuscripts hold so much information beyond just the text that they carry has led a growing number of scholars to argue for a renewed focus on the manuscripts themselves. These scholars operate under headings such as **Material Philology**, **Book History**, and **Ancient Media Criticism**, and they ask us to value manuscripts as more than just containers of good or bad readings. Approaching text-bearing objects as three-dimensional archaeological artifacts has brought about a fresh interest in manuscripts and a broader sense of what we can learn from them.

Increased access to online digital images of manuscripts has further directed attention to these objects as more than just carriers of texts. There is a growing recognition that transmission of texts was a fluid process, with the line between copying and composing often becoming blurred.

Moreover, each individual manuscript has an important story to tell, even if scholars of earlier generations might not have had a high opinion of the text carried on it. A manuscript may show you what a text with a long history of transmission looked like in one particular instantiation. Manuscripts may introduce you to the notes of active readers of the past and their interpretations of the text you are working on, they may provide hints at the contexts of engagement in which the embodied text took part, and they may enlighten you about the development of particularly salient variant readings.

The driving force behind *Working with Manuscripts: A Guide for Textual Scholars* is the conviction that knowledge of manuscripts is important for all interpreters of ancient texts. This book is not an introduction to Manuscript Studies—those introductions already exist. It is an invitation to students and scholars of ancient literary texts who already know the languages and are familiar with the texts from critical editions to include the study of manuscripts in their scholarship.

We have written the book with graduate students and early career scholars in mind, but we hope that it is helpful for anyone who wants to study a manuscript for the first time. With an awareness that the study of manuscripts may feel like

Introduction 7

an obscure and out-of-reach undertaking, we have envisioned this book as a hands-on guide to best practices. We try to demonstrate what you can gain by studying handwritten copies of ancient texts while we also signal some common pitfalls in this kind of work. Growing out of our own successes and failures, the book covers the whole research process, from considerations of **provenance**, ethics, and access to the practicalities of on-site research, analysis, and publication. Our guidelines have two prongs: Do not be intimidated by the idea of working with manuscripts, but at the same time, be aware of the necessary skills, customary processes, legal guidelines, and ethical challenges. *Working with Manuscripts* demystifies manuscript work.

The two authors of this book are textual and manuscript scholars. We were both originally trained in the study of ancient religions, but during the past fifteen years we have thoroughly integrated the study of manuscripts into our scholarship on texts. Liv has focused on late antique and medieval Syriac manuscripts, and Brent has focused on ancient and late antique Greek manuscripts. In keeping with our areas of specialization, this book includes examples from work on ancient, late antique, and medieval manuscripts, primarily those produced in the Middle East and the Mediterranean basin. Many of these manuscripts are commonly categorized as "Christian" in the sense that they were produced, used, and stored at institutions and by groups of individuals that self-identified as Christians (e.g., monastic milieus). However, in terms of textual transmission, these manuscripts carry texts that can be described as "Jewish," "Christian," or "classical." The advice we offer in this book is directed especially toward scholars working on these corpora of texts, but many of the practical tips we provide will be helpful to others as well.

Because of the past and ongoing effects of colonialism, many of the manuscripts we discuss are currently kept in

8   Introduction

institutions in Europe and the United States, so the majority of the collections to which we refer are based in these parts of the world. Access to manuscripts, like access to many resources, is unequally distributed throughout the globe. We return to the ethical and practical aspects of this situation in Chapter 3 and on several occasions throughout the book.

In the following chapters, we invite you to consider manuscripts as three-dimensional artifacts. We encourage you to explore manuscripts and to do so with the outlook of someone who is doing more than just reading texts. At the end of each chapter we offer suggestions for further reading. These sources can serve as good entry points for deeper research on topics that we address more briefly in this book. We have focused on resources written in English, although in some cases, when the best and most recent contributions are in Italian, German, or French, we include them too. The glossary at the end of the book contains some specialist terminology and technical terms (flagged in bold when they are introduced in the text) that may be useful to you as you read this book and, we hope, continue your work with manuscripts.

1

Manuscripts as Artifacts

Why should we study manuscripts, and what does such study involve? In this chapter, we briefly describe manuscripts as artifacts and begin to make a case for why scholars who interpret literary, "immaterial" texts should be interested in learning about the very material manuscripts that allow such texts to exist. (For a fuller demonstration of the kinds of things that textual scholars can learn from manuscripts, see Chapter 5.) The primary tools of the trade for manuscript production are writing surfaces, such as papyrus and parchment; inks; and styluses or other writing implements. These can be used to produce texts in different formats, such as the **roll** (scroll) and the **codex** (bound book with pages). Yet a material text is always more than just the words on the writing surface. Those words are written in a particular script and arranged in specific layouts that can affect interpretation. Indentation, punctuation, spacing, chapter breaks, and titles can all be informative.

Textual scholars are often very comfortable thinking about context—for instance, the social context in which a literary work is produced or the life of the author. Yet one of the key insights of Material Philology and Book History, among other perspectives, is that the literal, physical *con*text also matters. That is to say, the materiality of texts, along with the texts that surround your chosen text in a given manuscript, can provide insight into how the producers of your text understood the text they were copying. In addition to these aspects of the production of manuscripts, evidence of the usage of manuscripts in the years, decades, and centuries after their production can enrich the story of the text that is transmitted in the manuscript. Corrections, marginal notes, and signs of wear can all be informative. Paying attention to these kinds of material details can enhance the interpretation of a literary, "immaterial" text (Box 1.1).

BOX 1.1. Why Study Manuscripts? Books Are for More than Just Reading

In *Divining Gospel: Oracles of Interpretation in a Syriac Manuscript of John* (Berlin: De Gruyter, 2020), Jeff W. Childers explores a manuscript (London, British Library, Add. 17,119) that contains a copy of the Gospel of John. However, the pages of this sixth- or seventh-century manuscript also carry oracular statements (such as "In five days the matter will turn out well for you") interspersed in the gospel text. In critical editions, this manuscript has been used as just another witness to the Syriac text of the Gospel of John. Childers's study now shows that this particular manuscript was more than that: It had been produced to facilitate the practice of sortilege, a type of fortune-telling by drawing lots. The codex contains not only a gospel but also tools for divination.

Manuscript and Print

As we noted, this book is not an introduction to the technical study and editing of manuscripts. Some good examples of such books can be found in the Further Reading section at the end of this chapter. Nevertheless, we need to provide an overview of some of the basic vocabulary about manuscripts, at least as it applies to the most frequently encountered formats of ancient, late antique, and medieval Mediterranean and Middle East manuscripts: the roll and the codex.

We may define a manuscript as an inscribed object containing, among other things, text written by hand. Before the expansion of the printing press, the production of manuscripts was simply the way that texts circulated in the Middle East and the Mediterranean basin. People continued to produce manuscripts well after the introduction of print technology, and the production of manuscripts continues today in many communities—for example, in some groups who use Hebrew, Ethiopic, Syriac, or Arabic. In the era before automation, each step of the process of manufacturing a book was carried out by hand, from the preparation of the writing surfaces to the copying of the text. Thus, each individual manuscript is unique.

One of the most obvious differences between a printed text and a manuscript is often the handwritten script itself. As a person who can read printed texts of ancient languages with some fluency, you may find it a jarring experience to be confronted with a handwritten copy of a text you know that is written with unfamiliar letter forms and layout. One of the first challenges of working with manuscripts is becoming accustomed to deciphering a variety of different kinds of handwriting.

The study of ancient scripts is known as **paleography,** and it is a skill that you will need to develop somewhat to be able

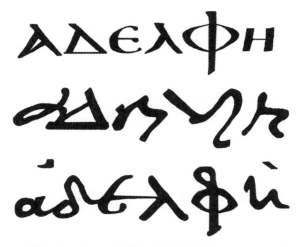

FIGURE 1.1. The Greek word ἀδελφή (*adelphē*) written in three distinct scripts—a majuscule (top), a cursive (center), and a minuscule (bottom). (Illustration by Brent Nongbri.)

to work comfortably with manuscripts. Sometimes scripts produced by hand can approach the regularity, consistency, and legibility of modern type, but in other cases, you may find writing in which individual letters have forms that are less familiar to you or that are connected to one another in surprising ways. You may also find that some words or phrases are regularly abbreviated. Figure 1.1 shows the Greek word ἀδελφή (*adelphe*) written in three distinct scripts, a formal **majuscule** (with neatly separated capitals), an informal **cursive**, and a formal **minuscule** (with less separated letters formed with more curves).

Scripts in all languages change over time, and conventions for printing ancient alphabets are often connected to the particular kind of script that was in use when and where the first printed editions were produced. The typefaces were designed to match the manuscripts that were available at hand.

The ability to efficiently read the more difficult scripts is a skill that comes only with time and with practice reading transcripts side by side with images of the manuscripts. For beginners, paleographic handbooks and charts of letter forms can be very helpful guides (Box 1.2). For more on paleography, see Chapter 5.

BOX 1.2. Examples of Paleographic Handbooks

Brown, Michelle P. *A Guide to Western Historical Scripts from Antiquity to 1600*. London: The British Library, 1993. This book provides an overview of Latin scripts.

Harrauer, Hermann. *Handbuch der griechischen Paläographie*. 2 vols. Stuttgart: Hiersemann, 2010. These volumes are mainly useful for cursive forms of Greek.

Hatch, William H. P. *An Album of Dated Syriac Manuscripts: With a New Foreword by Lucas Van Rompay*. Piscataway, NJ: Gorgias Press, 2012.

Turner, Eric G. *Greek Manuscripts of the Ancient World*. 2nd rev. ed. London: Institute of Classical Studies, 1987. This volume is more helpful for Greek manuscripts written in majuscule scripts.

Yardeni, Ada. *The Book of Hebrew Script: History, Palaeography, Script Styles, Calligraphy, and Design*. London: The British Library, 2002.

There is no comparable handbook of Coptic paleography produced in the past century. See the discussion in Anne Boud'hors, "Issues and Methodologies in Coptic Palaeography," in *The Oxford Handbook of Egyptian Epigraphy and Paleography*, ed. Vanessa Davies and Dimitri Laboury (New York: Oxford

---

BOX 1.2. *(continued)*

University Press, 2020), 618–633. Also see the relevant chapters of Alessandro Bausi et al. eds., *Comparative Oriental Manuscript Studies: An Introduction* (Hamburg: Tredition, 2015), open access: https://www.aai.uni-hamburg.de/en/comst/pub lications/handbook.html.

Many older paleographic handbooks are available through Internet Archive: Digital Library of Free and Borrowable Books, archive.org, such as Edward Maunde Thompson, *An Introduction to Greek and Latin Palaeography* (Oxford: Clarendon, 1912). There is much useful data in some of these older guides. Use them when necessary, but be aware that some of the theoretical approaches and vocabulary are outdated.

The Materials of Manuscripts

Many different kinds of physical media acted as support for writing: stones, bones, wooden boards, tree bark, clay, **ostraca** (potsherds), **lamellae** (thin metal sheets), waxed wooden tablets, and more. The most common media for the transmission of literature were papyrus and parchment; later it was paper, which was developed in China perhaps as early as the first century CE but was not widely used in the Middle East and the Mediterranean world until several centuries later.

Papyrus is a writing surface produced from stalks of the *Cyperus papyrus* plant, which grew abundantly in Egypt in the Nile delta region throughout antiquity and the medieval era. The mature stalks were cut down and the hard outer casing removed. The softer inner pith was then cut into thin strips. To make a sheet, several of these strips were set side by side on a

Manuscripts as Artifacts

flat surface to form a first layer. Then a second layer of strips was placed on top of the first but oriented perpendicularly. When the two layers were pressed together and dried under pressure, the drying juices from the plant bonded the layers. The result was a flat sheet, called a *kollēma,* with the fibers on the two faces oriented at right angles to one another. The fibers could be flattened to improve the writing surface by rubbing the papyrus with a smooth bone or shell.

Parchment is produced from animal hides, usually those of a sheep, goat, or calf. The term **vellum** is sometimes reserved for especially fine calfskin but is also sometimes used as a synonym for "parchment." After obtaining animal hides, parchment makers soaked the pelts in a chemical bath and then, stretching the wet skins over molds, laboriously removed the hair and the fat with a blunt blade. The cleaned skins were rinsed and dried under tension, with additional scraping to even the surfaces and remove blemishes. The resulting parchment could be trimmed to different sizes to fit the needs of bookmakers. The two faces of a parchment sheet have different qualities. The side from which the hair was removed ("the hair side") can be identified by the presence of hair follicles and often a more yellow color. The side from which excess meat and fat was removed ("the flesh side") generally has a whiter color and is somewhat less receptive to inks because of residual fats in the skin.

Like papyrus, **paper** is a plant-based product, but manufacturing paper is very different from manufacturing papyrus. Paper is produced using pulp, which is obtained either directly from plants or indirectly from plant-based products like linen or cotton cloth. The plants or textiles are first broken down by a process called **maceration**. The plant material is shredded into small pieces, put into a container with water, and then (literally) beaten to a pulp. Maceration frees the cellulose fibers in the plant material to mix thoroughly with the water. A sieve-like screen or a cloth in a frame (a mold) is then dipped into the solution and lifted out, in the process capturing a thin layer of the cellulose fibers suspended in the liquid. The mold is lightly shaken to create an even layer of pulp as the excess water drains through the mold. This layer of pulp is laid out on a cloth, pressed, and dried. Sheets can be made in different sizes and shapes by using different molds. Sheets are further refined through **sizing**, the process of applying starch, gelatin, or other materials to the paper to make its surface less porous and thus less likely to allow ink to bleed. (For the experience of writing on unsized paper, try to use a marker to write on toilet paper.)

The most common inks used with papyrus and parchment were black inks made with a base of water and gum arabic (the hardened sap of the acacia tree) combined with either soot or metallic salts and oak galls ("iron gall" inks). Well-prepared soot or carbon inks are dark black. Iron gall inks are also very dark black when they are applied, but over time, they can fade to a brown color, which is how this type of ink is generally recognized now by scholars who study ancient and medieval manuscripts. Other colors used for decoration or illumination were derived from a variety of pigments.

In the ancient and late antique Mediterranean and Middle East, inks were generally applied using a quill pen or a stylus cut from a reed. At a later period, it is unclear exactly when, metal nibs came into use. Writing on both papyrus and parchment could be erased by using a sponge wet with water or by scraping with a blade, or some combination of the two. If an entire area of writing was erased and then re-inscribed, the resulting manuscript is known as a **palimpsest**, from the Greek *palimpsēstos* ("scraped again").

Rolls and Codices

Rolls could be made of animal hide or papyrus. When animal hide was used, individual rectangular sheets of the desired size were cut from prepared skins and stitched together with thread, usually with the hair side used as the writing surface, which was prepared for inscribing by lightly incising **ruling** lines to guide the writing. The back of the roll was generally left blank, and the roll was wound up with the writing on the inside surface, protected from damage.

Papyrus rolls were made of individual sheets of papyrus (*kollēmata*) that were pasted together with a slight area of overlap (a ***kollēsis***); they were usually pasted left over right when employed with a left-to-right writing system like Greek or Latin (Figure 1.2). It is easier to write along horizontal fibers, so it was this surface of the roll that was usually inscribed. Thus, the side with horizontal fibers is generally called the "front" of a papyrus roll. The back side of the roll was usually left blank. The top and bottom of the closed roll are each called the *frons* (plural *frontes*). Luxury rolls were sometimes wrapped around a wooden rod (*umbilicus*) that had nobs (*cornua*) extending above and below the *frons*.

Typically, the first sheet of a roll was left blank. This blank sheet, called a ***prōtokollon,*** served as a cover for the roll when it was wound up. Given this protective function, the *prōtokollon* was usually pasted to the back side of the roll, making the first *kollēsis* of the roll right over left (see Figure 1.2). Writing was generally arranged in columns of varying length that were planned by lightly ruling the papyrus using lead. These ruling lines are rarely visible on surviving papyri but are mentioned by ancient authors, and their presence has been confirmed by scientific testing. For prose texts, the written columns often form precise geometric shapes (rectangles or parallelograms).

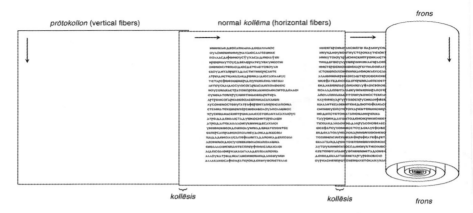

FIGURE 1.2. Diagram of a papyrus roll containing a copy of Book 1 of the *Iliad*. (Illustration by Brent Nongbri.)

For poetic texts, the appearance of the columns shows greater variation. The length of a poetic line often determined the length of the column (see Figure 1.2). The length of the lines in the columns of prose texts were purely up to the aesthetics of the copyists. In the case of papyrus rolls, columns of writing often crossed the joins between sheets (*kollēseis*), but the stitched joins of parchment rolls usually prevented writing across multiple sheets.

While the hair side of parchment and the horizontal fibers of papyrus make the superior writing surface, it is not that much more difficult to write on the flesh side of parchment or the vertical fibers of papyrus. Thus, in some rare instances rolls were inscribed on both sides. Such rolls are called **opisthographs**. On other occasions, the back side of a roll that had been used to copy one text was reused at a later time for a different writing task. Such rolls are sometimes also called opisthographs in the secondary literature, but it is better to reserve

Manuscripts as Artifacts

that term for rolls that use the front and back surface for the same act of writing. If two distinct writing acts are in view, it is best to call the manuscript a reused roll.

A codex is a more complicated physical object than a roll. With a roll, we are dealing with an essentially two-dimensional writing surface that only gains a significant third dimension when that surface is rolled up. With a codex, we are dealing with several different parts that work together to form the artifact. The writing surface is cut into sheets that are stacked and folded. One of these folded sheets is called a **bifolium** or **bifolio** (plural bifolia), and each of the two resulting leaves is called a **folium** or a **folio** (plural folia). Each face of the folio is called a **page**. The bifolia can be stacked in one large pile and folded to form a **quire** (sometimes called a **gathering**), which can be bound together by looping one or more **tackets** (cords) through holes pierced in the central fold of the quire (Figure 1.3). Or the bifolia can be stacked into several smaller piles. Each pile is then folded to form a small quire, and the quires are sewn together using thread (Figure 1.4). In principle, quires can be made up of any number of bifolia (Box 1.3).

Because both sheets of papyrus and sheets of parchment have different surfaces on their two faces (hair and flesh on parchment, horizontal fibers and vertical fibers on papyrus), bookmakers often arranged quires so that when they were folded, like surfaces faced each other. The first modern scholar who noted this phenomenon in parchment codices was Caspar René Gregory (1846–1917), and it is thus known as **Gregory's Rule**.

The assembled codex has a vocabulary all of its own. Different specialists may sometimes use differing terminology, but the basic vocabulary we provide here should serve you reasonably well (for a highly detailed lexicon, see The Language of Bindings website: https://www.ligatus.org.uk/node/712). The

FIGURE 1.3. Model of a single-quire codex composed of one stack of folded papyrus bifolia and bound by a single thread tacket with a parchment stay (a thin stiffening strip) protecting the central fold. (Model and photo by Brent Nongbri.)

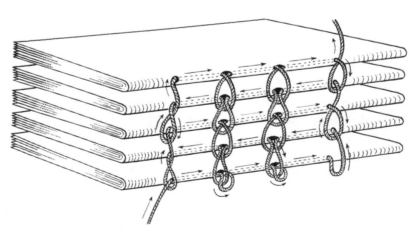

FIGURE 1.4. Diagram of a multi-quire codex showing the stitching of the quires. (Image adapted from Jean Vezin, "La réalisation matérielle des manuscrits latins pendant le haut Moyen Âge," in *Codicologica 2: Eléments pour une codicologie comparée,* ed. Albert Gruys and J. P. Gumbert [Leiden: Brill, 1978], 38, Figure 2.)

Manuscripts as Artifacts

BOX 1.3. The Makeup of Quires

Specialists sometimes use different names to refer to quires made up of specific numbers of bifolia:

one bifolium	*unio* or *union* (plural *uniones*)
two bifolia	*binio* or *binion* (plural *biniones*)
three bifolia	*ternio* or *ternion* (plural *terniones*)
four bifolia	*quaternio* or *quaternion* (plural *quaterniones*)
five bifolia	*quinio* or *quinion* (plural *quiniones*)
six bifolia	*senio* or *senion* (plural *seniones*)

The most commonly found types of quires are *quaterniones* (from which the English word "quire" is derived), followed by *terniones* and *quinones*. Quires of seven or more bifolia do exist, but they are less frequently designated by a specific term.

top of the codex is called the **head**, and the bottom is called the **tail** (Figure 1.5). The bound side of the quire or set of quires is the **spine**, and the opposite end is the **fore edge**. Some codices have **endbands** sewn on to the head and the tail of quires to protect their edges. The bound stack of quires can be most clearly identified as the **book block**; it is sometimes referred to as the "text block," but as we will see, this phrase is also employed in another way.

Figure 1.6 is a schematic diagram of an **opening** of a codex. The two visible folia contain the Vulgate translation of the end of Genesis, marked here with an **explicit**, and the beginning of Exodus. For manuscripts containing Greek, Latin, or other languages read left to right, we call the left page of an opening the **verso** and the right page of the opening the **recto**.

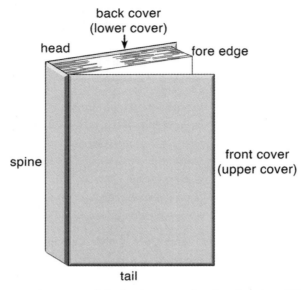

FIGURE 1.5. Diagram of the basic parts of a closed codex. (Illustration by Brent Nongbri.)

For manuscripts written in Arabic, Hebrew, or other languages read right to left, we reverse these labels: the recto is on the left and the verso is on the right. These terms are also sometimes used to mean the "front" and "back" of single sheets or rolls of papyrus or parchment, but such usage can be confusing and should be avoided.

The written area of the codex page is called the **text block**. It can consist of one or several columns of writing. The folia of papyrus codices were sometimes lightly pierced with four holes—one in each corner—to define the limits of the text block; the holes are called **prickings**. Parchment codices were similarly pricked and also frequently ruled by lightly incising ruling lines, guidelines to help the copyist keep the text properly aligned. The blank areas surrounding the text block are

Manuscripts as Artifacts

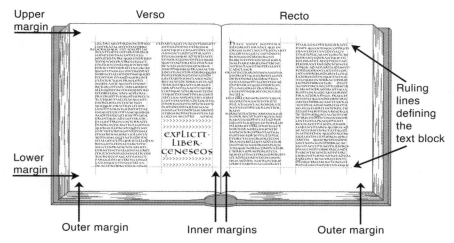

FIGURE 1.6. Diagram of an open codex containing portions of the Vulgate (Latin) text of Genesis and Exodus. (Illustration by Brent Nongbri.)

the margins. The inner margin (the area near the fold) is sometimes called the **gutter**. The outer margins are generally wider than the inner margins, and the lower margins usually larger than the upper margins. Margins can also be used for other kinds of writing, as we discuss below.

Most codices had covers of some kind, although in the case of the earliest codices and codex fragments, these covers have only rarely survived. The oldest covers were composed of layers of pasted papyrus—sometimes blank papyri, sometimes inscribed papyri that were being reused. These layers were wrapped in leather or parchment. Several of the Coptic books known as the Nag Hammadi codices, likely produced in the fourth or fifth century CE, had their leather covers intact when they appeared on the antiquities market in Cairo in the 1940s (Figure 1.7).

FIGURE 1.7. The open leather cover of Nag Hammadi Codex V after the removal of the papyrus quire, showing the remains of wrapping cords at the edges, the protective wrap-around flap (left), the spine-lining strip (center), and remains of the papyrus stuffing (right). (Photo by Basile Psiroukis. Image courtesy of the Institute for Antiquity and Christianity Records, Special Collections, Claremont Colleges Library, Claremont, California.)

If a cover contains used papyri, as some of the Nag Hammadi covers did, the information on this waste papyrus can sometimes provide clues about when and where a codex was manufactured or rebound (Box 1.4). At a later stage, the use of wooden boards as covers became more common, although these boards were still often fully or partly wrapped in leather. By the medieval period, covers were sometimes richly decorated with metal fittings, clasps, paintings, and precious stones. In some codices a folium was pasted to the inside of each cover (**pastedowns**).

Manuscripts as Artifacts

BOX 1.4. Why Study Manuscripts?
Clues Hidden in Covers

In *The Monastic Origins of the Nag Hammadi Codices* (Tübingen: Mohr Siebeck, 2015), Hugo Lundhaug and Lance Jenott argue that Egyptian monks produced and read the Nag Hammadi codices. In contrast to scholars who treat the Coptic texts in these codices mainly as late translations of earlier Greek originals, Lundhaug and Jenott focus on the evidence for production and use of the manuscripts themselves. They note, for instance, that the waste papyrus used to make the cover of one of the codices included many letters written by and/or addressed to monks, a strong argument for suggesting that monks were involved in the manufacture of these manuscripts and that the codices were meaningful for monks in a late-antique Egyptian monastic setting (see Figure 1.7).

The description of codex manufacture outlined here is generally applicable, but as handcrafted artifacts, each ancient codex presents its own idiosyncrasies of construction. In addition, the earliest surviving codices are often heavily damaged or have undergone various repairs and rebindings, so understanding the details of their construction can be quite challenging. Over the years, Brent has found that making models of ancient books can be very useful for gaining a greater understanding of how codices were put together. He has produced models of several early codices using papyrus, parchment, and leather; one of them is pictured in Figure 1.3. This kind of model making is time consuming (though very enjoyable), but the process need not be so involved. Sometimes just using some scrap paper to make a simple mock-up of a confusing quire can be a helpful exercise in understanding the structure of a codex.

Much more could be said about the materials and manufacture of ancient manuscripts, and the Further Reading list at the end of this chapter is a good place to begin looking if you are interested. But this basic introduction is all that you need to begin thinking about the ways that paying attention to manuscripts can enrich the study of ancient texts.

Layout, Organization, and Structure

Manuscripts are carriers of texts. Here we will look more closely at the different forms of texts that you may encounter on the pages of a manuscript and the way that texts are distributed in the manuscript. In addition to texts, we will also look briefly at illuminations, decorations, symbols, and other readers' aids. First, we deal with the layout of the individual page. Second, we turn to features that aid the organization of a specific work inscribed in the manuscript. And third, we explore traces of the overall structuring of the manuscript. The aim of this section is to equip you with the information you need to understand what you see on the manuscript page. However, it includes only the most basic information, and we encourage you to consult the resources that we have listed in the Further Reading section below.

The layout of the page (sometimes referred to by the French *mise en page*) concerns the physical embodiment of the text on the page. Layout has to do with the proportion of the text block relative to the total size of the page, the breadth of the four margins at top, bottom, and sides of the page, the number of columns on the page, and the number of lines in each column. One of the main functions of the page layout is visual order and readability. Before the copyist inscribed the text on the page, the text block was commonly prepared for writing by pricking and ruling, as we noted earlier. The text in the text block is usually organized in the shape of columns. Most codices contain one or two columns of text on each page. On other occasions, the text can be ordered in a three- or even four-column layout.

The margins, the areas of the page that fall outside the text block, can be different sizes, depending on the format and the value ascribed to the manuscript, as well as the time and tradition in which the manuscript was produced. The margins play an important role. Since the outer edges are the most vulnerable parts of a folium, the margins protect the text block from, for example, soiling and decay. Some margins carry no or little text; others may include texts and symbols inscribed there either by the producers or by later active readers of the manuscript. The uninscribed areas between the columns in a multicolumn layout are called **intercolumns**.

Many of the phrases and nonverbal marks in manuscripts are features that aid the organization of a specific work or parts of that work. These **paratexts** guide readers in different ways. Some can signal the beginning or end of a work as well as its various subsections. This visual organization of the text can help the reader navigate. Copyists could, for instance, use inks of a different color to mark out the first letter or word of a new work or section (this is sometimes called **rubrication**); they commonly used red ink in contrast to the more usual black or brownish-black ink of the text. In other instances, **titles** identify the work. The title may be located in the beginning and/or at the end of the text, and it was also commonly inscribed in red ink, larger letters, and/or letters in a different style of writing. Sometimes those who produced the manuscript also added decorations, such as wavy lines or configurations of dots and lines, to titles or initial words and letters. To mark the end of one work and the beginning of the next, copyists frequently skipped one or more lines, leaving a space.

28   Manuscripts as Artifacts

Sometimes interlaces or bands or other decorative features fill these empty spaces. In some manuscripts, illuminations may also mark the beginning of a work or collection or the transition from one work or collection to the next.

Copyists had different ways of marking out subsections of works. Some subsections were identified with subsection headings. **Delimitation markers** are symbolic marks that communicate the beginning, the end, or a pause in a sense unit or a reading unit. For example, dots or rosettes can mark the end of a sentence, a paragraph, or a unit intended for public reading. Or the first lines of subsections can be either indented or projected slightly into the margins; the latter feature, called **ekthesis**, is shown in some of the lines in Figure 1.6. You may come across many other systems of delimitation in the manuscripts you study, among them different arrangements for identifying chapters and liturgical readings. These features can add important dimensions to the interpretation of the main text (Box 1.5).

Some of the marks, sequences of words, and phrases in codices have yet another function: to communicate the correct structure of the codex to binders (and to readers). For example, **quire signatures**, which helped the binder arrange the quires in the right order, typically appear in the margins of the first and/or last page of a quire. The pages of codices were only occasionally numbered at the time of production. Page numbers became more helpful as a reference tool in the age of the printing press, when multiple copies of a book were produced with identical text on each page. More often, the folia of ancient and medieval codices were numbered by modern owners. **Foliation** usually involves a number and a letter—for example, 125v, meaning the verso side of the 125th folio. Such a system of reference overcomes the problem of having no page numbers or having multiple sets of page numbers within a given codex.

Manuscripts as Artifacts

> **BOX 1.5. Why Study Manuscripts? Tales Told by Titles**
>
> In *Manuscripts of the Book of Revelation* (Oxford: Oxford University Press, 2020), Garrick V. Allen explores the Greek manuscripts that transmitted Revelation, focusing on titles and other paratexts that accompany the text. Allen argues that manuscripts served as sites of interpretation and that, for scholars today, paratexts offer windows into past interpretations of Revelation. The variety of titles preserved in the manuscripts show how those who produced them identified the book of Revelation at various stages of its history, and additional notes in the margins indicate how some later readers interpreted key sections of the text. Allen shows how a study of paratexts may provide an important, and far too often overlooked, source for the ongoing history of the reception of Revelation.

Voluntary Signs of Use and Involuntary Traces of Handling

Our brief description of the layout of the page and the various types of texts you will encounter focused on the manuscript as an object of production. In other words, we focused on the outcome of the activities of the copyist and the production team. However, it may be just as interesting to explore the manuscript as an object of circulation, focusing on the texts and marks that later active readers left there. Most (if not all) manuscripts were made in order to be used, and the current condition of those that survive shows that they were indeed handled and read. Manuscripts that came into the hands of new readers often changed in some ways, and these changes are part of the history of the artifact.

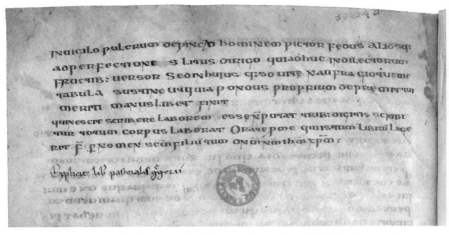

FIGURE 1.8. The last inscribed page of a codex of Christian works showing a colophon by the copyist as well as later marks and inscriptions: Paris, Bibliothèque nationale de France, lat. 9561, fol. 81 verso. (Image courtesy of the Bibliothèque nationale de France, Paris.)

A first category of traces left in manuscripts by active readers are voluntary traces of use, such as **marginalia**—things like **scholia**, annotations, and **doodles**—and erasures. Although the role of margins is to protect the text inscribed in the text block, margins themselves may contain text. We have already mentioned quire signatures and foliation. Many margins also contain other types of text. Some glosses and liturgical notes were inscribed by the producers of the manuscripts, and sometimes a copyist also added a **colophon**, which is a formulaic note containing information about the time, place, and occasion of the copying or a direct address to the reader (Figure 1.8 and Box 1.6).

Other short phrases could have been added in the postproduction phase. Such additional notes can be ad hoc stand-alone notes, elaborate series of notes running through a manuscript, or anything between those two poles. They can be

Manuscripts as Artifacts

31

BOX 1.6. Examining a Colophon

Figure 1.8 shows the last inscribed page of an eighth-century parchment codex containing a set of Christian works in Latin and concluding with the *Regula pastoralis* attributed to Pope Gregory I. After the body of the text, the copyist added a short colophon (lines 6–8 in this image):

> qui nescit scribere laborem esse n(on) putat trib(us) digitis scribitur, totum corpus laborat. Orate p(ro) me qui istum libru(m) legerit. F(init) p(er) nomen s(an)c-(tu)m filiu(m) tu(u)m d(omi)n(u)m n(ostru)m Iē(su)m Xr(istu)m.

Roughly translated, it reads: "Only someone who doesn't know how to write thinks it's easy. Three fingers do the writing, but the whole body toils. If you're reading this book, pray for me. It is finished. Through the holy name, your son, our Lord Jesus Christ."

Another hand, writing in a later script, has added, "Explicit liber pastoralis Gregorii," or "Here ends the book of Gregory's [*Regula*] *pastoralis.*" Finally, we see the circular collection stamp of the Bibliothèque nationale with the almost illegible script "Bibliotheque Royale" surrounding a crown and three fleurs-de-lis.

The writer of the colophon has used several abbreviated forms, usually marked with a horizontal line above the shortened portion of the word. Note that the copyist has used some Greek characters in the name "Jesus Christ," even while retaining the Latin case endings (IHM XPM). Note also at the top of the image, a later writer has written (upside down relative to the text on the page) a short alphabetic exercise ("a b c d e f").

inspired by and relevant to the texts in their proximity—most commonly, the text in the text block—or they can be motivated by other concerns and be less obviously relevant to the text with which they share the page. The distribution and amount of additional notation vary greatly, depending on, for example, the type of collection and the cultural tradition of which the manuscript and the readers were a part. Some of the most common notes are corrections, marks highlighting special contents, additional markers of unit division in places where a later reader saw fit to add them, phrases facilitating use of a passage or prescribing a special reading practice, prayer notes, and notes stating ownership or other relationships with the physical object.

When Liv first started working on manuscripts, she was surprised to find that quite a few of the Syriac manuscripts she explored contained doodles, pen trials, and writing exercises. She was working on biblical manuscripts at the time, and she had no idea that scribes and active readers sometimes treated them as notepads. If you imagine all manuscripts to be venerable objects, you, too, may be in for a surprise. In many traditions, scribbles and rough drawings are relatively common. Open spaces in the margins or on guard sheets or other blank pages may, for example, contain traces of someone testing the pen or offering additional adornments. Some high-quality drawings may also appear. Some are related to the contents of the text in the text block; others are not. Many drawings belong to a set repertoire of motifs. Bird and animal drawings and floral and vegetal motifs are among the most frequent.

Not only did copyists sometimes erase their work to correct mistakes while they were producing manuscripts, but later users of manuscripts also erased by scraping or using a sponge. These later acts of erasure could take place in order to change or correct perceived errors in the text or to eliminate some or all of the earlier writing in order to prepare the writing surface for reuse (Figure 1.9).

FIGURE 1.9. St. Catherine's Monastery, Arabic Manuscripts 589, fol. 20v, including a partly erased area. This codex contains 2 Baruch and 4 Ezra in Arabic. The erased lines probably contained a description of the fallen angels (2 Bar. 56). This is the second of two erasures that occur in sections containing contested contents. It is possible that this is the reason why these words were erased. (Image courtesy of the Library of Congress Collection of Manuscripts in St. Catherine's Monastery, Mt. Sinai.)

A second category of traces that you will probably come across in the manuscripts you study are involuntary signs of physical handling. Among the most common are traces of thumbing, burn marks, wax stains, and traces of saliva or sweat (Figure 1.10).

Traces of thumbing are common in a manuscript that was in use over a long period of time; the traces basically show

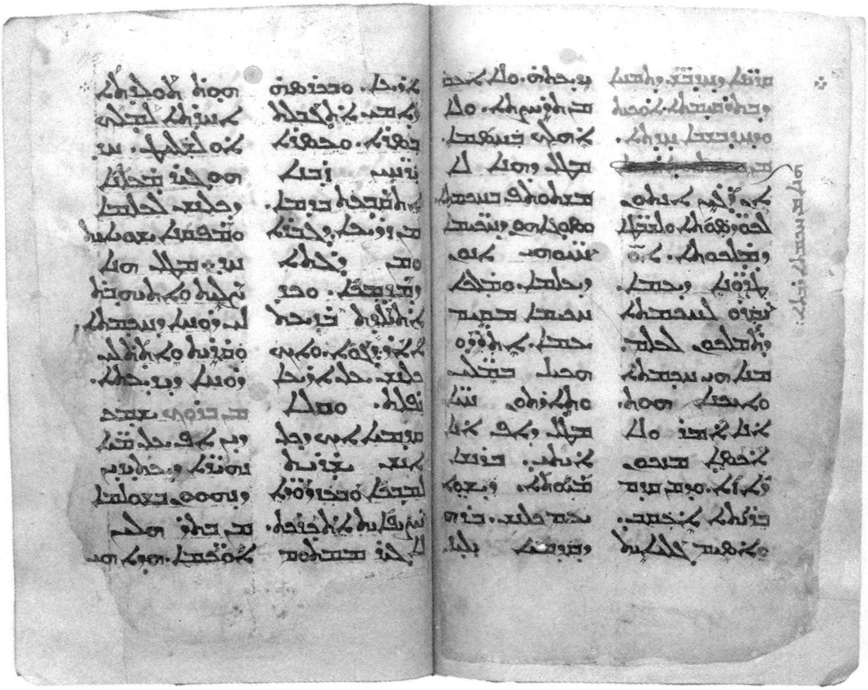

FIGURE 1.10. This Syriac lectionary manuscript displays several voluntary and involuntary traces of handling: wax stains (upper margins and intercolumns); traces of fluid spills and attempts to wipe them away (recto page [left page in the image], left column); additional vowel signs (all columns); and an erasure and correction, presumably the work of the copyist (verso page [right page in the image], right column). The lower outer margins are worn and repaired. Also note that this image is a composite of separate images of the pages digitally joined using software: Folios 174v and 175r of London, British Library, Add. 14,687. (Image © The British Library Board.)

Manuscripts as Artifacts

that people before you handled the codex and that sometimes their hands were less than clean when doing so. Sometimes you may come across fully formed fingerprints, but more often the visible result of the many hands that touched the manuscript is just a grimy, gray area. In a codex, the highest density of these involuntary signs of handling is typically found on the outer and lower margins of the page. This is where readers touched the folio to turn the page. Indeed, experience with and expectation of thumbing may be one of the reasons why those who produced the manuscript made room for generous margins in the first place and also why the lower and outer margins are sometimes more generous than the inner and upper ones. The producers knew that without wide margins, handling would soil or smear the text in the written area.

Manuscripts were often read indoors with less than ideal sources of light, usually oil lamps and candles. It is no wonder, then, that some manuscripts contain burn marks. These burn marks can be of different sizes but are generally recognizable as organically shaped holes with charred rims. The use of candles also resulted in wax stains. If left intact, wax is observable as a well-rounded transparent yellow substance, a palpable drop on the manuscript page. On most occasions, though, the wax substance was removed by the person responsible for the wax accident, a later reader, or a conservator, and all that is left is an oily stain that is visible on both sides of a parchment or paper folio (Box 1.7).

Human bodily fluids can leave their mark on manuscripts as well. Some readers read the text on manuscripts vigorously and out loud, resulting in sprays of spittle on the page. Other readers hunched over manuscripts in deep concentration, often in uncomfortably warm settings, which could result in drips of sweat on the page or sweaty hands handling the manuscript. Either of these practices could leave manuscripts stained with

BOX 1.7. Decay and Conservation

Decay is an unavoidable part of the life of a manuscript, and you will probably come across evidence of it in the manuscripts you study. Moisture and mold have left their marks in many manuscripts. Some have been damaged by insects and pests. Heavy handling may lead to slits in the edges of folia, and if the spine of a codex breaks, individual bifolia and even entire quires may go missing. Owners who have cared for these manuscripts over the years have often attempted to repair them and to stop processes of decay with various degrees of success. You may come across the results of these historical attempts at preservation, for example, in the form of stitching or adhesive tape. For a good introduction to contemporary principles and practices of preservation of manuscripts, see Abigail Bainbridge, ed., *Conservation of Books* (London: Routledge, 2023).

traces of fluid, which could cause local ink smears. Attempts to wipe these away could smear the ink even more.

Tracing thumbing, burn marks, wax stains, and signs of fluids can be a valuable exercise in its own right. For example, you may learn which part of a manuscript readers engaged with most frequently.

Learn from Professional Codicologists and Papyrologists

Specialists in **codicology** and **papyrology** spend years gaining expertise in their fields. You cannot expect that kind of mastery unless you invest the necessary time and effort. Yet you don't have to be a fully fledged codicologist to include the study of manuscripts in your textual research. What you do need is some knowledge about the world of manuscripts and some familiarity with its basic vocabulary. You can gain some of these basic skills with the resources we have introduced to you. Use the Further Reading section to learn more.

Further Reading

INTRODUCTIONS TO PAPYROLOGY AND MANUSCRIPT STUDIES

Agati, Maria L. *The Manuscript Book: A Compendium of Codicology*. Translated by Colin W. Swift. Studia Archaeologica 214. Rome: L'Erma di Bretschneider, 2017.

Bagnall, Roger S., ed. *The Oxford Handbook to Papyrology*. New York: Oxford University Press, 2011.

Bausi, Alessandro, ed. *Comparative Oriental Manuscript Studies: An Introduction.* Hamburg: Tredition, 2015. Open access: https://www.aai.uni-hamburg.de/en/comst/pub lications/handbook.html.

Clemens, Raymond, and Timothy Graham. *Introduction to Manuscript Studies.* Ithaca, NY: Cornell University Press, 2007.

Maniaci, Marilena. *Breve storia del libro manoscritto.*Rome: Carocci editore, 2019.

MATERIAL PHILOLOGY

Allen, Garrick V. *Manuscripts of the Book of Revelation: New Philology, Paratexts, Reception.* Oxford: Oxford University Press, 2020.

Cerquiglini, Bernard. *Éloge de la variante: Histoire critique de la philologie.* Paris: Editions du Seuil, 1989.

Childers, Jeff W. *Divining Gospel: Oracles of Interpretation in a Syriac Manuscript of John.* Manuscripta Biblica 4. Berlin: De Gruyter, 2020.

Lied, Liv Ingeborg. *Invisible Manuscripts: Textual Scholarship and the Survival of 2 Baruch.* Studien und Texte zu Antike und Christentum 128. Tübingen: Mohr Siebeck, 2021.

Lied, Liv Ingeborg, and Hugo Lundhaug, eds. *Snapshots of Evolving Traditions: Jewish and Christian Manuscript Culture, Textual Fluidity, and New Philology.* Texte und Untersuchungen zur Geschichte der altchristlichen Literatur 175. Berlin: De Gruyter, 2017.

Lundhaug, Hugo, and Lance Jennott. *The Monastic Origins of the Nag Hammadi Codices.* Studien und Texte zu Antike und Christentum 97. Tübingen: Mohr Siebeck, 2015.

Nichols, Stephen G. "Introduction: Philology in a Manuscript Culture." *Speculum* 65 (1990): 1–10.

Zumthor, Paul. *Essai de poétique médiévale.* Paris: Editions du Seuil, 1972.

MATERIALS

Christiansen, Thomas. "Manufacture of Black Ink in the Ancient Mediterranean." *Bulletin of the American Society of Papyrologists* 54 (2017): 167–195.

Holsinger, Bruce. *On Parchment: Animals, Archives, and the Making of Culture from Herodotus to the Digital Age.* New Haven: Yale University Press, 2023.

Hunter, Dard. *Papermaking: The History and Technique of an Ancient Craft.* 2nd ed. New York: Knopf, 1947.

Lewis, Naphtali. *Papyrus in Classical Antiquity.* Oxford: Clarendon Press, 1974.

Lewis, Naphtali. "Papyrus in Classical Antiquity: A Supplement." *Papyrologica Bruxellensia* 23 (1989): 9–42.

Lewis, Naphtali. "Papyrus in Classical Antiquity: An Update." *Chronique d'Égypte* 67 (1992): 308–318.

Reed, Ronald. *Ancient Skins, Parchments and Leathers.* London: Seminar Press, 1972.

Willi, Anna. *Writing Equipment.* Vol. 2 of *Manual of Roman Everyday Writing.* Nottingham, UK: The LatinNow Project, 2021. Open access: https://library.oapen.org/handle/20.500 .12657/56668.

ROLLS

Johnson, William A. *Bookrolls and Scribes in Oxyrhynchus.* Toronto: University of Toronto Press, 2004.

Turner, Eric G. "The Terms Recto and Verso: The Anatomy of the Papyrus Roll." In *Actes du XVe Congrès International de Papyrologie,* ed. Jean Bingen and Georges Nachtergael, 1–71. Brussels: Fondation Égyptologique Reine Élisabeth, 1978.

CODICES

Andrist, Patrick, Paul Canart, and Marilena Maniaci. *La syntaxe du codex Essai de codicologie structurale.* Bibliologia 34. Turnhout, Belgium: Brepols, 2013.

Boudalis, Georgios. *The Codex and Crafts in Late Antiquity.* New York: Bard Graduate Center, 2018.

Miller, Julia. *Meeting by Accident: Selected Historical Bindings.* Ann Arbor, MI: The Legacy Press, 2018.

Petersen, Theodore C. *Coptic Bookbindings in the Pierpont Morgan Library,* ed. Francisco H. Trujillo. Ann Arbor, MI: The Legacy Press, 2021.

Szirmai, Ján A. *The Archaeology of Medieval Bookbinding.*
Aldershot, UK: Ashgate, 1999.

Turner, Eric G. *The Typology of the Early Codex.* Philadel-
phia: University of Pennsylvania Press, 1977.

LAYOUT

Martin, Henri-Jean, and Jean Vezin, eds. *Mise en page et
mise en texte du livre manuscrit.* Paris: Éditions du Cercle
de la Librairie, 1990.

ADDITIONAL NOTES AND TRACES OF HANDLING

Lied, Liv Ingeborg, and Marilena Maniaci, eds. *Bible as
Notepad: Tracing Annotations and Annotation Practices in
Late Antique and Medieval Biblical Manuscripts.* Manu-
scripta Biblica 3. Berlin: De Gruyter, 2018.

Rudy, Katryn M. "Dirty Books: Quantifying Patterns of Use
in Medieval Manuscripts Using a Densitometer." *Journal
of Historians of Netherlandish Art* 4 (2010): 1–44.

CONSERVATION

Bainbridge, Abigail, ed. *Conservation of Books.* London:
Routledge, 2023.

Parodi, Laura E. "Conservation and Preservation." In *Comparative Oriental Manuscript Studies: An Introduction,*
ed. Alessandro Bausi, 539–563. Hamburg: Tredition, 2015.

2

Finding Your Manuscript

Once you have determined that you need to consult a manuscript, how do you find out where it is physically located? To see a manuscript in person, you will need to find the institution where the manuscript is kept and determine the **shelfmark**, the unique identifier used by the holding institution in sorting their materials. Finding this information can be a very simple process. In the best cases, the common name of a manuscript can tell you everything you need to know—for example, "London, British Library, Papyrus 131." In other cases, however, seeking out the physical location can be surprisingly difficult and not at all intuitive. With Google and other web search engines, locating a particular manuscript has become a great deal easier than it was a century or even a decade ago. Google can often be a helpful first step, and you may well find all the information you need right away. But Google and other search engines can also become time-sucking rabbit holes that yield fruitless results.

This chapter will introduce you to other sources that may streamline your search. Several online tools can help you locate a manuscript, but in some cases you may still have to learn to use a variety of print resources to locate a particular manuscript or a particular part of a particular manuscript. We offer a bit of instruction in using these tools, but the main point is simply to make you aware of their existence. We have been selective in the resources that we discuss, focusing on our own areas of interest and training, but our suggestions for further reading can provide more leads.

In the current period of fast technological change, **union catalogs**, which allow searches for manuscripts across multiple collections, are becoming more common. Databases that collect cataloging data and make it easily searchable are on the rise. With the expansion of such projects, many of the tips in this chapter may be obsolete in just a couple of years. We hope that happens sooner rather than later. But until that time, we offer this chapter as an aid.

How Can Locating a Manuscript Be So Hard?

Locating a manuscript can be challenging for several reasons. From almost the moment manuscripts are produced, they are moved. They are usually easy to carry, and throughout history, some of them were seen as valuables that could be sold, stolen, or serve as gifts. The physical form of manuscripts could also change as ownership shifted. Some codices were divided into smaller bound units. Yet others grew as users merged one or more **codicological units.**

These processes of movement and change continue today for manuscripts that pass through the antiquities market. Among the unfortunate effects of the antiquities market is the splitting of manuscripts among multiple institutions, meaning that a single manuscript might find homes in multiple places. Dealers often divide manuscripts, especially codices, and sell the dismembered parts to different buyers. This process of destruction and confusion can begin at the time of the discovery of a manuscript or at the first meeting between historical

Finding Your Manuscript

wardens and potential buyers and continue throughout a manuscript's time on the market.

If a particular manuscript is important to your studies, you will probably want to know the place or places where it is physically located. Finding out might not be a straightforward process. For example, a copy of a commentary on the Psalms written by Didymus the Blind (ca. 313–398 CE) was found in Egypt in 1941 but was immediately split up and sold to different buyers. If you were interested in consulting a particular page of this manuscript, you would first need to determine whether it was in the part of the book that ended up in Cairo, Cologne, Geneva, London, or Provo, Utah, in the United States.

A second reason why locating manuscripts can be hard has to do with the customary ways of naming manuscripts. Manuscripts can change names, and today many of them have one or more nicknames along with their shelfmark. In addition, several naming and reference systems exist side by side. Sometimes a single manuscript may be called by many different names, and sometimes similar designations may refer to different manuscripts, depending on context. This situation is further complicated by the many sets of cryptic abbreviations that scholars use to discuss manuscripts, especially papyri: you could be forgiven for not knowing that JdE 88745 is the same manuscript as Publ.Sorb.Pap. 1.683. This is an important point to learn early on: Manuscripts can be known by catalog numbers, publication numbers, or shelfmarks—or by all three! If a manuscript has been moved from one collection to another, or if a collection has redesigned its ordering system, a manuscript may even be known by several shelfmarks. To see a manuscript in person, you need to find the institution where the manuscript is located right now, and you need to figure out its current shelfmark.

A third challenge is that many catalogs, reference works, databases, and editions organize their materials with reference to texts (individual works) and the collections or genres to which scholars believe that these texts belong. This means that the texts are not ordered with reference to discrete manuscripts or, if the manuscript is fragmentary, to discrete, minimal entities, such as single leaves or fragments. For example, a **miscellaneous codex** that includes some biblical texts and some commentary literature may be split in the catalog even though these parts were copied by the same copyist and exist together in the same manuscript. This kind of cataloging practice was applied to William Wright's catalog of the Syriac manuscripts in the British Museum (now: British Library). Wright's catalog proceeds according to genres, not shelfmarks. This method of organization prompted Elizabeth Reif and Michael Penn to put together "The Wright Decoder," which provides an index that helps you maneuver through the catalog in search of the manuscripts.

So, how can you find the kind of information you need about a manuscript? A number of resources can help.

Some Tools for Locating Manuscripts

The tools that organize the study of manuscripts are immensely useful, but they can be more than a little intimidating. They are arranged in many different, overlapping ways. Lists, databases, and catalogs can be based on language, writing surface, contents of the texts, and more. These tools also often rely on many different sets of abbreviations. The vast sea of abbreviations and numbers encountered in the study of manuscripts can be especially challenging for newcomers. In what follows, we will work through some different examples that involve different tools that can help you determine the physical location of a manuscript and also become familiar with some of the naming and abbreviation conventions that you will surely encounter in your work. The digital resources outlined in Box 2.1 are

Finding Your Manuscript 45

BOX 2.1. Some Digital Tools for Locating Manuscripts

Unfortunately, there is no one-stop database for all manuscripts. Since manuscripts from different cultures and time periods require many different kinds of expertise, the tools designed to facilitate the study of manuscripts tend to vary by discipline. Here are a few places to start.

For medieval manuscripts of all kinds:

- The Schoenberg Database of Manuscripts at the University of Pennsylvania (https://sdbm.library.upenn.edu/) aggregates data about premodern manuscripts from library, museum, and private collections, as well as auction catalogs.

For ancient and late antique manuscripts in Greek, Latin, Hebrew, Demotic, and Coptic:

- The resources gathered at the Trismegistos site (TM for short, https://www.trismegistos.org/index.php) can be very helpful. Especially useful is the Leuven Database of Ancient Books (LDAB, https://www.trismegistos.org/ldab/), where you can search for particular manuscripts using several different criteria and arrive at a page with useful data and a bibliography. These resources are only available by subscription. If you are affiliated with an academic institution, you can check your library's resource page, either in the main catalog or under "Databases," to see if you have institutional access. These databases contain a great deal of information, but they are not entirely intuitive and require some practice for effective use.

For Greek manuscripts:

- The Pinakes database (https://pinakes.irht.cnrs.fr/) aggregates the Greek holdings of many catalogs but does not list papyrus manuscripts.

BOX 2.1. *(continued)*

For Latin manuscripts:

- The digital edition of Paul O. Kristeller's *Latin Manuscripts before 1600,* 4th rev. and enlarged edition (Munich: Monumenta Germaniae Historica, 1993), contains a list of printed catalogs and unpublished inventories of manuscript collections (https://www.mgh-bibliothek.de/kristeller/index.html).
- The website Earlier Latin Manuscripts (https://elmss .nuigalway.ie/) focuses on manuscripts of Latin literary texts produced before the year 800.

For Coptic manuscripts:

- The suite of resources at the PAThs database, Tracking Papyrus and Parchment Paths: An Archaeological Atlas of Coptic Literature, especially the section entitled "Manuscripts" (https://atlas.paths-erc.eu/manuscripts).

For Syriac manuscripts:

- The collection of open access resources at syri.ac (https:// syri.ac/), syriaca.org (https://syriaca.org/index.html), and e-ktobe (https://www.irht.cnrs.fr/fr/ressources/base-de-don nees/e-ktobe).
- The 60,000-plus images of the Vööbus Syriac Manuscript Collection hosted by the Hill Museum and Manuscript Library (https://hmml.org/).

usually the best places to start, but we will refer you to several print resources as well. Some of these are quite expensive, but most can be found in good academic libraries. You can find the full bibliographic details for the print resources we mention in the Further Readings at the end of the chapter.

Finding Your Manuscript

EXAMPLE 1

Let's say you have been working on the Greek text of the book of Ezekiel, which is full of interesting textual variations from the Hebrew text. You notice in the **apparatus** of the critical edition you are using an especially intriguing textual variant in the manuscript called 967. This is the Rahlfs number, that is, the number of the manuscript in the list of Septuagint manuscripts established by Alfred Rahlfs (1865–1935). You would like to have a closer look at this textual variant and perhaps others that might be similar to it in the same manuscript. Turning to the list of witnesses in the introduction to the critical edition, you find that 967 is a papyrus codex containing a copy of Ezekiel, Daniel, Susanna, and Esther. A little further reading alerts you to the fact that this codex was broken up after its discovery and sold to several different institutions. How do you efficiently determine the physical location of the pages that interest you? It would be ideal if there were a single modern edition of all the parts of this ancient book, but unfortunately, such a resource has not yet been produced. In this case, since you are dealing with a relatively early papyrus manuscript containing works from the Septuagint, a good resource to consult is Detlef Fraenkel's *Verzeichnis der griechischen Handschriften des Alten Testaments*. This resource is arranged geographically by collection, but you can look up the Rahlfs number in the index, which directs you to the entries for the locations where the different parts of the manuscript are held (in Dublin, Köln [Cologne], Madrid, Montserrat, and Princeton). In this case, if you look at the entry for the first location listed under the index entry for 967 (Dublin), you find a convenient listing of which folia are found at each institution.

If you are unable to find a copy of this book, there are other resources that have information, but they may not be as up-to-date or as easy to use. For instance, you could consult

48 Finding Your Manuscript

Kurt Aland's *Repertorium der griechischen christlichen Papyri I, Biblische Papyri: Altes Testament, Neues Testament, Varia, Apokryphen.* Again, you can begin by looking up Rahlfs number 967 in the index. And again, you will find yourself directed to several different sections in the book. This resource, like so many others, is centered on the texts contained in manuscripts rather than on the manuscripts themselves. The result is that information about one single physical codex is divided up in accordance with the biblical books it contains. So you will need to look at the separate entry for the portion of this manuscript that contains Ezekiel, and there you can learn the different locations of all the extant folia.

As you might have noticed from the title of the last resource, *Repertorium der griechischen christlichen Papyri,* this book provides similar information for papyrus manuscripts that contain other kinds of early Christian literature in Greek. But it is current only up to 1976. For manuscripts published more recently, you will need to turn to online sources that may not contain such thorough information. For manuscripts containing texts of the New Testament, there are ample digital resources that can answer most of these kinds of questions, primarily the online Kurzgefasste Liste maintained by the Institute for New Testament Textual Research in Münster (Institut für Neutestamentliche Textforschung, INTF, http://ntvmr.uni-muenster.de/liste). For manuscripts of the Septuagint, you can turn to the latest version of the list of manuscripts maintained by the Academy of Sciences in Göttingen (last updated in 2012); the Academy is now named Niedersächsische Akademie der Wissenschaften zu Göttingen. The information at the Academy is not as detailed as it is at the other resources we have named, but it can be helpful in determining the physical location of your manuscript. For apocryphal Christian literature, the e-Clavis: Christian Apocrypha project of the Medieval

Academy of America can often provide good leads and bibliography (https://www.nasscal.com/e-clavis-christian-apocrypha/). For Greek manuscripts of all kinds, the Pinakes database is very helpful (https://pinakes.irht.cnrs.fr/).

EXAMPLE 2

Now consider a case in which you are working on a text by the Jewish philosopher Philo of Alexandria. You notice a reference to the earliest manuscript containing your text, the Oxyrhynchus codex of Philo, and in particular you see the claim that multiple different copyists worked together on this volume. You would like to compare the hands for yourself, so you want to see the manuscripts.

If you have made it this far in your study of the Oxyrhynchus Philo, you have probably already noticed that its pieces have several different identifiers: P.Oxy. 9.1173, P.Oxy. 11.1356, P.Oxy. 18.2158, P.Oxy. 85.5291, PSI 11.1207, and P.Haun. 1.8. Abbreviations like these are very common ways of referring to the publications of different manuscripts, particularly papyrus and parchment manuscripts from Egypt. For Greek and Latin manuscripts from Egypt and elsewhere, you can find an organized set of common abbreviations online: *Checklist of Editions of Greek, Latin, Demotic, and Coptic Papyri, Ostraca, and Tablets* (https://papyri.info/docs/checklist), which also provides links to editions that are available online through repositories like the Internet Archive (archive.org). This resource would allow you to quickly learn that these abbreviations refer to the following publication series:

> P.Oxy.: The Oxyrhynchus Papyri
> PSI: *Papiri greci e latini* (Pubblicazioni della Società
>   Italiana per la ricerca dei papiri greci e latini in Egitto)

50 Finding Your Manuscript

P.Haun.: *Papyri Graecae Haunienses* (that is, Greek
papyri at Haunia [the Latin name of Copenhagen])

The first number following the abbreviation is usually the
number of the volume in the series, and the second number is
usually the number assigned to the specific manuscript or fragment. So, you now know the editions of these manuscripts.
How can you discover their physical location?

You may already associate the famous collection of Oxyrhynchus papyri, excavated by Bernard Grenfell and Arthur
Hunt from 1896 to 1907 on behalf of the Egypt Exploration
Fund, with the Bodleian Art, Archaeology, and Ancient World
Library at Oxford University (formerly known as the Sackler
Library). The majority of the Oxyrhynchus papyri are indeed
there. But not all of them. Some of the first P.Oxy. pieces to be
published were subsequently given to the various donors to
the Egypt Exploration Fund. These donors included both
large universities and museums and smaller institutions like
seminaries and secondary schools, mostly in the United Kingdom and the United States. Other papyri from Oxyrhynchus
emerged during excavations that took place after 1907—for
instance, by Italian teams that dug at Oxyrhynchus in the
1920s and the 1930s. But archaeologists were not the only ones
digging at Oxyrhynchus. Antiquities sellers also had workers
active at the site, so some papyri found at Oxyrhynchus ended
up on the antiquities market.

The Oxyrhynchus codex of Philo falls into all three of
these categories. The first parts of the codex to be published,
P.Oxy. 9.1173 and P.Oxy. 11.1356, were excavated by Grenfell and
Hunt's team and were all subsequently distributed to donor
organizations. In this case, they did not travel far. They were
given to the Bodleian Library at Oxford and can still be found
there today. The piece excavated by the Italian team (PSI

Finding Your Manuscript

11.1207) is now in the Biblioteca Medicea Laurenziana in Florence. P.Haun. 1.8 is in the SAXO Institute at the University of Copenhagen. The other two P.Oxy. pieces, P.Oxy. 18.2158 and P.Oxy. 85.5291, remain in the Bodleian Art, Archaeology, and Ancient World Library in Oxford.

Where can you find this kind of information? Since this manuscript happens to contain works of the Jewish philosopher Philo, the best place to go is Joseph van Haelst's *Catalogue des papyrus littéraires juifs et chrétiens*. In this one-volume work, you can look up Philo in the index and find the information for this manuscript as item 696.

We also run into another naming issue here. The catalog of van Haelst is itself part of a series—Paris-Sorbonne Série "Papyrologie" 1, produced by Publications de Sorbonne—and sometimes items in his catalog are referred to by their entry number. So you might see this codex of Philo referenced as Publ.Sorb.Pap. 1.696.

We have made this point before, but it is worth emphasizing: A single manuscript can be known by many different names, catalog numbers, publication numbers, or shelfmarks. In the case of the Philo codex, because it is made up of several pieces at different institutions (and hence with different shelfmarks) that were published in different series (and hence with different publication names), you can see how it might make sense to refer to all the fragments collectively by a catalog or database number. If, however, you're interested in actually seeing a manuscript or part of a dismembered manuscript in person, you will need to track down the shelfmark of the part that interests you, since this is the designation that you will need to provide the owning institution.

The information collected in van Haelst's volume is convenient, but you again run up against the limits of print resources, since it is current only up to 1976. Some manuscripts have moved since that time, and many more manuscripts have been published. P.Oxy. 85.5291, for instance, was published in 2016, so it is not mentioned by van Haelst. In this case, the websites associated with these collections can provide more current data. For items published in the P.Oxy. series, there is a convenient online "Location-List" (https://oxyrhynchus.web.ox.ac.uk/location-list). For items in the PSI series, a searchable database provides location information at PSIonline (http://www.psi-online.it/). For the Copenhagen papyrus collection, there is a very sparse but still helpful homepage (https://aigis.igl.ku.dk/bulow/PHaun.html).

EXAMPLE 3

Let's imagine that you are writing a monograph on the Old Testament book of Susanna. You come across previous research saying that the Syriac Peshitta version has copies of this book in different collection contexts—for instance, together with Daniel, as part of the *Book of Women* and as part of the collection called *Maccabees*. You become fascinated and want to know how Susanna is located and identified in Syriac manuscripts in these contexts and whether and how location and identification change over time. In other words, you aim for an overview of the preserved Peshitta manuscripts. How can you achieve a comprehensive overview of these manuscripts, and how can you find their location?

Since the 1960s, the *List of Old Testament Peshitta Manuscripts (Preliminary Issue)*, edited by the Peshitta Institute (then in Leiden, now in Amsterdam) has been the obvious place to go if you want to find a Syriac Peshitta Old Testament manuscript. Even in the 2020s, the *Peshitta List* is a good place to start. It provides a convenient overview of the manuscripts that were known in the early 1960s. To be precise, it lists the

Finding Your Manuscript

manuscripts that were used by the teams working on the editions of the Peshitta Old Testament. These editions were to be published by the International Organization for the Study of the Old Testament and the Leiden Peshitta Institute. In the *Peshitta List* the manuscripts are ordered by location (town or monastery), collection, shelfmark, and a dedicated **siglum** consisting of numbers and letters.

Although this additional siglum may add to the confusion of the multiple naming systems of manuscripts, it is also immensely helpful. The siglum offers information about the proposed century of production and the type of manuscript and gives a sequence number that keeps it apart from other similar manuscripts datable to the same century. For example, the siglum 8a1 tells you that the manuscript was produced in the eighth century, that it is a **pandect** (a codex containing a full Bible), and that it is the first of a sequence of other pandects in the list dating to the eighth century.

The *Peshitta List* also offers indices that order the manuscripts by works. In other words, a quick look at this list has already offered you a lot of help in finding manuscripts containing Susanna and in identifying their contents and location.

However, as the title of the list suggests, the *Peshitta List* is not comprehensive; the editors knew more manuscripts were out there. The list also contains a few mistakes. As the editors' knowledge about documents grew, they offered updates in the "Peshitta Institute Communication," first published in the journal *Vetus Testamentum* (1962–1999) and then in the *Journal for the Aramaic Bible/Aramaic Studies*. Some of these updates were added to new printed editions of the *Peshitta List*.

As time has passed, and particularly as the overview of Syriac manuscripts in collections in the Middle East has improved, several new Peshitta manuscripts have come to light. To find these manuscripts, you will have to use both print and digital resources. Two print resources may help you. A good first stop is Alain Desreumaux's *Répertoire des bibliothèques et des catalogues de manuscrits syriaques* (written with Françoise Briquel Chatonnet). It gives you an overview of the locations of manuscripts known to Desreumaux at the time of publication (1991) and lists several important print catalogs. However, as his overview stops in the early 1990s, you have to move on. An updated, annotated list of catalogs of Syriac manuscripts compiled by André Binggeli appears in *Comparative Oriental Manuscript Studies: An Introduction,* edited by Alessandro Bausi et al.

The digital portals syri.ac (https://syri.ac/), syriaca.org (https://syriaca.org/index.html), and e-ktobe (https://www.irht .cnrs.fr/fr/ressources/base-de-donnees/e-ktobe) offer invaluable overviews and direct links to online catalogs and manuscripts that are digitally available. Indeed, several collections with large holdings of Syriac manuscripts have made manuscripts available online since the mid-2010s. For example, this is the case with many manuscripts in the Bibliothèque nationale de France (Paris), the Cambridge University Library, the Biblioteca Ambrosiana (Milan), and the Biblioteca Apostolica Vaticana (Rome/Vatican). The Hill Museum and Manuscript Library (HMML) has also made several manuscripts digitally available, particularly manuscripts kept in Middle Eastern collections (https://hmml.org/).

At the time of writing, there is no union catalog of Syriac manuscripts. David Michelson is currently developing such a catalog to be published on syriaca.org after 2026. This tool is likely to revolutionize the process of searching for these manuscripts. However, it is not yet live. If your aim is to get an overview of the Peshitta manuscripts that contain Susanna, you still have to work your way through a print list (in various editions), updates in print journals, recent print catalogs, digital repositories, and online portals. You will find out that the manuscripts are spread throughout Europe and the Middle East, that Syriac copyists copied the book in a variety of contexts, and that the manuscripts date from the sixth through the twentieth century.

The search for Susanna in Syriac manuscripts while longing for a comprehensive overview shows the challenges of working on a manuscript tradition where the mapping of manuscripts is still in progress. It also reflects the joy and complexity of studying a living manuscript tradition. Although print was introduced to the Syriac tradition centuries ago, there are still some copyists who continue to produce handwritten books.

EXAMPLE 4

Let's return now to the manuscript of Didymus the Blind. As we mentioned, the codex containing his *Commentary on the Psalms* was divided up on the antiquities market in the 1940s and has been dispersed in collections around the world. If you want to consult a particular folium in this manuscript, you need to know where it is. For papyrus manuscripts of early Christian authors writing in Greek, the go-to resource is Kurt Aland and Hans-Udo Rosenbaum, *Repertorium der griechischen christlichen Papyri II: Kirchenväter-Papyri*. This work is arranged alphabetically by ancient author. If you look up Didymus the Blind, you find several different papyri, including the manuscript of his Psalms commentary. Aland and Rosenbaum provide a full breakdown of which pages are located in each of the five different repositories in the five different countries where the manuscripts are held. You also find other catalog designations of the manuscript, a very detailed codicological discussion, and an ample bibliography up to the publication date of 1995. For the manuscripts that it contains, this book is a superb resource.

EXAMPLE 5

As a final short case study, imagine you are working on the fragmentary Dead Sea Scrolls papyri from Cave 7 at Qumran. You are aware that several of these fragments contain bits of legible text that have yet to be positively identified with any known pieces of literature. You may notice that the handwriting on some of these fragments looks similar, but there are no obvious fits among the fragments in terms of their physical shape or the words written on them. Since papyrus fibers provide unique patterns that run on both sides of the writing surface, you may want to see the back sides of the fragments to check for matching patterns of fibers. Unfortunately, the published photographic plates and digital images online show only the front sides of the fragments. How might you consult the manuscripts themselves?

Those who study the Dead Sea Scrolls benefit from an entire body of scholarship and many tools that help with navigating the corpus of scrolls and fragments. A good place to start is with the bibliographic resources at the Orion Center of the Hebrew University of Jerusalem, http://orion.mscc.huji.ac.il/index.html. Yet, one of the most basic pieces of data, the physical location of a particular fragment, can be tricky to ascertain. The Dead Sea Scrolls are most closely associated with the Shrine of the Book at the Israel Museum in Jerusalem, and indeed the vast majority of the Dead Sea Scrolls are kept there, but some scrolls and/or fragments are also held at other locations, including Amman, Paris, Oslo, and New Jersey. The Trismegistos online database provides these locations, but the locations can also be found in print resources like Emmanuel Tov's *Revised Lists of the Texts from the Judaean Desert,* which informs you that the fragments from Cave 7 are indeed at the Israel Museum in Jerusalem, along with the majority of the Scrolls; they are framed together as plate 789.

When Your Manuscript Is Lost or Destroyed

After you consult the relevant resources, you could discover that the manuscript that interests you is nowhere to be found. Manuscripts do get misplaced or even destroyed. For instance, we mentioned the "Location-List" for items published in *The Oxyrhynchus Papyri* series. If you browse through this list, you will find that thirty-one manuscripts are labeled "Lost," over seventy are described as "Not found" or "Not yet found," and an additional eleven are labeled "Destroyed?" To take another example, the Lying Pen of Scribes project has identified over one thousand small fragments of the Dead Sea Scrolls that were known at one time but have since been lost.

How might manuscripts be lost or destroyed? Loss can happen, for example, through neglect or by way of unfortunate circumstances. When staffing changes happen at collections, a gap can appear in the chain of institutional memory, and artifacts can be misplaced. In fact, some degree of loss is to be expected in large collections that have existed over long periods of time. Most collections have items that have been displaced, stolen, or not properly cataloged. Manuscripts also sometimes "disappear" when they are sold. Auction houses often conduct so-called private treaty sales: the manuscripts are sold secretly and out of the public eye.

Manuscripts can be destroyed in the same ways that any object can be destroyed. Natural disasters such as floods and earthquakes can destroy manuscripts. Bombing during World War II damaged or destroyed many manuscripts and other cultural heritage items. Since the 1990s, warfare in the Middle East has also put many manuscripts at risk of destruction. Fragile papyrus and parchment can be destroyed by neglect and by ongoing chemical decay. And accidents sometimes happen. In discussing the mounting of an especially delicate

58 Finding Your Manuscript

Coptic papyrus codex of the fifth century containing the *Kephalaia* of Mani (a Christian teacher of the third century CE), the conservator Rolf Ibscher relates the following story: "The remains of the Berlin *Kephalaia* had escaped destruction [during and after World War II] by being stored in my house after 1945. . . . Unfortunately a marvelous leaf, after being separated [from the book block], was lost, completely obliterated. I had to sneeze, but could not turn away with lightning speed—and all had disappeared without a trace."[1] This fragile papyrus folium that contained part of an otherwise unknown ancient text was lost to an unlucky sneeze before anyone could read it: the sneeze turned it to dust.

So what do you do when, despite your best efforts, you cannot establish the current whereabouts of a manuscript or you learn that it has been destroyed? For seemingly lost manuscripts, it can be helpful to contact curators at the institution of its last known whereabouts. Most libraries and museums have contact forms or a dedicated email address for questions. Get in touch and inform the curator what you are looking for. Provide all the relevant information you have: What shelfmarks or other inventory number(s) do you know? Where did you see this manuscript referenced? Briefly describe the research you have done, so the curator does not have to repeat your work. Even a curator who cannot locate your manuscript may provide you with helpful tips. When you are at a collection, ask the staff whether they have uncatalogued materials in their archives. Very often this is the case. You might get lucky. After all, lost manuscripts are sometimes found.

For manuscripts that have been destroyed, your options are more limited. For papyrus and parchment manuscripts from Egypt, there is an extensive photographic archive housed at the Centre de Documentation de Papyrologie Littéraire

(CeDoPaL, https://www.cedopal.uliege.be/cms/c_7615320/en/cedopal). You can contact the staff there to request images for study purposes. Archival photos of the Dead Sea Scrolls can be found at the Leon Levy Dead Sea Scrolls Digital Library (https://www.deadseascrolls.org.il/?locale=en_US). The Peshitta Institute harbors microfilms of a large number of Syriac manuscripts, some of which have been lost or destroyed. Many of the resources named in this chapter and listed in the Further Readings also provide bibliographies, which sometimes give an indication of where photographs of a given manuscript have been published.

Moving Ahead

Hopefully, the resources we have outlined in this chapter can help you find the physical location of the manuscript that you want to consult. Our goal has been to try to make your search as efficient as possible, but you may be forced to do some trial-and-error searching of your own. This is perfectly normal. The overlapping systems of naming can be frustrating in the early stages of your work with manuscripts. Dealing with all the abbreviations for publications and collections is a bit like learning a foreign language—or, rather, like learning several foreign languages simultaneously. Remember that learning a new field is a slow process. And there is still more to do. The next step after finding the current location of your manuscript is digging into its history.

Further Reading

Aland, Kurt. *Repertorium der griechischen christlichen Papyri I, Biblische Papyri: Altes Testament, Neues Testament, Varia, Apokryphen.* Berlin: De Gruyter, 1976.

Aland, Kurt, and Hans-Udo Rosenbaum. *Repertorium der griechischen christlichen Papyri II: Kirchenväter-Papyri.* Berlin: De Gruyter, 1995.

Bausi, Alessandro, ed. *Comparative Oriental Manuscript Studies: An Introduction.* Hamburg: Tredition, 2015. Open access: https://www.aai.uni-hamburg.de/en/comst/publications/handbook.html.

Binggeli, André. "Catalogues of Syriac Manuscripts." In *Comparative Oriental Manuscript Studies: An Introduction,* ed. Alessandro Bausi et al., 502–504. Hamburg: Tredition, 2015. Open access: https://www.aai.uni-hamburg.de/en/comst/publications/handbook.html.

Bruckner, Albert, and Robert Marchal, eds. *Chartae Latinae antiquiores: Facsimile Edition of the Latin Charters Prior to the Ninth Century.* 49 vols. Olten, Switzerland: U. Graf, 1954–1998.

Conway, Melissa, and Lisa Fagin Davis. "Directory of Collections in the United States and Canada with Pre-1600 Manuscript Holdings." *Papers of the Bibliographical Society of America* 109 (2015): 273–428.

Depauw, Mark, and T. Gheldof. "Trismegistos: An Interdisciplinary Platform for Ancient World Texts and Related Information." In *Theory and Practice of Digital Libraries—TPDL 2013 Selected Workshops,* ed. Łukasz Bolikowski et al., 40–52. Communications in Computer and Information Science 416. Cham, Switzerland: Springer, 2014.

Desreumaux, Alain, with Françoise Briquel Chatonnet. *Répertoire des bibliothèques et des manuscrits syriaques.* Paris: Éditions du Centre national de la recherche scientifique, 1991.

Fraenkel, Detlef. *Verzeichnis der griechischen Handschriften des Alten Testaments von Alfred Rahlfs, Bd. I, 1. Die Überlieferung bis zum VIII. Jahrhundert.* Septuaginta Vetus Testamentum Graecum Auctoritae Academiae Scientiarum

Gottingensis editum: Supplementum. Göttingen: Vandenhoeck and Ruprecht, 2004.

Gippert, Jost. "Catalogues and Cataloguing of Oriental Manuscripts in the Digital Age." In *Comparative Oriental Manuscript Studies: An Introduction,* ed. Alessandro Bausi et al., 531–537. Hamburg: Tredition, 2015.

Hægeland, Signe Marie. "Lost Dead Sea Scroll Fragments: A Database and Analysis of the Losses." Master's thesis, MF Norwegian School of Theology, Religion and Society, 2023.

Kristeller, Paul Oskar. *Latin Manuscript Books before 1600: A List of the Printed Catalogues and Unpublished Inventories of Extant Collections.* 4th ed. Munich: Monumenta Germaniae Historica, 1993.

Lowe, Elias Avery, ed. *Codices Latini antiquiores: A Palaeographical Guide to Latin Manuscripts Prior to the Ninth Century.* 12 vols. Oxford: Clarendon, 1934–1971.

Orlandi, Tito. "The CMCL Clavis Coptica: On Producing a Standardized List of (Coptic) Works and Manuscripts." *Comparative Oriental Manuscript Studies Bulletin* 4 (2018): 107–114. Open access: http://doi.org/10.25592/uhhfdm.265.

Peshitta Institute, Leiden University, ed. *List of Old Testament Peshitta Manuscripts (Preliminary Issue).* Leiden: Brill, 1961.

Reif, Elizabeth, and Michael Penn. "The Wright Decoder: A Page Index to the Catalogue of Syriac Manuscripts in the British Museum." *Hugoye* 16 (2013): 37–92.

Ricci, Seymour de. *Census of Medieval and Renaissance Manuscripts in the United States and Canada.* 3 vols. New York: H. W. Wilson, 1935–1940, with a *Supplement* by W. H. Bond published in 1962.

Richard, Marcel. *Répertoire des bibliothèques et des catalogues de manuscrits grecs.* 2nd ed. Paris: Centre national de la

recherche scientifique, 1958. Open access: https://www
.persee.fr/doc/dirht_1636–869x_1958_cat_1_1.

Tov, Emanuel. *Revised Lists of the Texts from the Judaean Desert*. Leiden: Brill, 2010.

van Haelst, Joseph. *Catalogue des papyrus littéraires juifs et chrétiens*. Université de Paris IV Paris-Sorbonne Série "Papyrologie" 1. Paris: Publications de Sorbonne, 1976.

3
Provenance and Why It Matters

Now that you have found where your manuscript is presently located, the next question to ask is: How did it get there? Thinking about manuscripts as more than just carriers of disembodied texts entails thinking about them as physical artifacts that have a life story. Somehow the manuscript that has caught your attention moved from the time and place where it was produced to the place where it is now. Sometimes this movement might be as small as a shift from one room in a monastery to another room in the same monastery. Other cases involve several moves across the globe and several changes in possession or claimed ownership. A key part of studying manuscripts is learning the story of these movements and changes. This is what we mean by provenance.

In this chapter, our aim is to guide you through an aspect of the study of manuscripts that has become hotly debated in recent years. In the nineteenth and twentieth centuries, knowing exactly where your manuscript came from was nice, but it was not considered terribly important, much less essential. What is sometimes called **provenience**, the origin or place of production of a manuscript, was generally considered more important than the provenance. But as more and more cultural-heritage professionals and scholars have become concerned about both the legality and the ethics of the ways that museum and library collections were assembled, the question of provenance has come to the forefront. In choosing to study manuscripts, you are opening yourself up to an exciting world of discovery but also to a world that can present some legal and ethical questions. Many people who study manuscripts (and many people who don't) hold *very* strong views on these questions. Although we will make our opinions on these debates clear, our goal is not to make you pick a side but rather to introduce you to some of the issues and to make sure that your decision-making is reasonably well informed.

The Colonial History of Manuscripts

Many of the manuscripts you want to study are currently kept in institutions in Europe and the United States. This may seem a bit odd, because many of them obviously originated elsewhere. Yet their present location is not a coincidence. Rather, it is the direct result of the global history of colonialism. The period from the sixteenth century through the middle of the twentieth century saw the transfer of large numbers of manuscripts from the Middle East, Africa, Central Asia, and elsewhere to Europe and, later, to the United States.

Over the centuries, European countries—England, Spain, France, Russia, Italy, and others—built empires and established military and administrative control over large parts of the world. The power structures that these empires established created a unidirectional flow of art and other cultural artifacts, even entire buildings, from the colonies to the European capitals. Included in this large-scale transfer were many manuscripts. On some occasions, manuscripts were legally bought

Provenance and Why It Matters   65

from or gifted by their former stewards. On other occasions, terms like "brought" and "gift" and "transfer" conceal historical practices that might more accurately be described as "deceit" and "exploitation" or even "pillaging" and "theft." Even in cases when a transaction was between seemingly equal partners, the larger historical picture shows that the former owners of the manuscripts tended to end up as the losing parties; for several accounts of these kinds of interactions, see the stories gathered at the "Manuscript Hunters" website, https://www.manuscripthunters.gwi.uni-muenchen.de/.

Many of the manuscripts that entered Europe became the treasures of newly established state museums and libraries and thus part of the nation-building enterprises of European states. Acquisition signaled the aspiration to power. The practice of collecting artifacts from all around the globe reflected a view among Europe's elite that they alone had the intellectual and moral capacity to act as curators and interpreters of the universal knowledge of the world (Figure 3.1).

Many modern academic disciplines were established in the colonial era and depend explicitly or implicitly on the exploits of European empires. Among them are disciplines with a focus on the manuscripts and literary texts of antiquity, such as Biblical Studies. The manuscripts that were brought to Europe make up a large part of these disciplines' source materials and were vital to the inception and development of these fields of study. Biblical scholars were also sometimes manuscript hunters and collectors.

Today the artifacts that were once brought to Europe and the United States are still in the museums and libraries of these countries, but debates about ownership and repatriation loom large. Some institutions have repatriated parts of their collections or plan to do so in the near future. Others hold on to them.

FIGURE 3.1. Spiridione Roma, *The East Offering Its Riches to Britannia* (London, British Library, Foster 245). This painting (oil on canvas) was commissioned in 1778 by the East India Company and adorned the ceiling of the Revenue Committee room at their London headquarters, East India House. Roma's allegorical painting depicts India and China offering valuable gifts to Britannia (Britain). (Image © The British Library Board.)

Why Be Interested in Provenance?

You may ask yourself why the life story of a manuscript matters. After all, you may be interested in something that a copyist or a user of a manuscript wrote two thousand years ago. If you can read it now, what difference does it make where the manuscript has been in the intervening centuries? Broadly speaking, there

Provenance and Why It Matters

are at least three ways to answer this question. First, these stories can sometimes dramatically change your view of your own research question. For instance, learning that your manuscript passed through the hands of several specific readers who made annotations on it might cast new light on the topic of your study. Second, you may discover that your manuscript is "too good to be true"—that is, it might turn out to be something other than it seems to be. The high-profile case of the so-called *Gospel of Jesus' Wife,* in which a respected scholar did not carry out a thorough investigation of provenance and ended up publishing a modern forgery, provides a cautionary tale. Likewise, the Dead Sea Scroll–like fragments that started to appear on the antiquities market after 2002 would not have mistakenly passed as genuine if the scholars who published them had vetted their provenance information. Third, digging into the provenance of your manuscript may alert you to potential legal and ethical issues that you need to consider before proceeding. It is this third aspect that will be our focus.

Different manuscripts have different kinds of life stories. Some of them have been in the same libraries from the time they were produced until the present. Others were discarded or forgotten for a decade or a century or a millennium after they were written and only recently rediscovered. A manuscript might have been stolen from a monastic library or legally sold to a visitor. A manuscript may have been legally excavated from an archaeological site, or it may have been looted. A manuscript may have been legally exported from the area where it was produced, or it might have been smuggled out. You do yourself a favor by doing all that you can to know these kinds of details about the manuscript that interests you.

Manuscripts can be looted, stolen, or smuggled because in addition to their historical, aesthetic, and cultural value, they also have a monetary value. One outcome of the academic study of manuscripts is a potential increase in this monetary value. For example, a papyrus codex containing unidentified Coptic texts is said to have sold for about $300,000 in the year 2000. After a scholar identified one of the texts in it as a copy of the *Gospel of Judas,* it sold just a year later to another private dealer for a reported $2.5 million.

Manuscripts have been bought and sold as commodities for centuries, but only relatively recently have scholars come to appreciate both the loss of knowledge that the trade in antiquities can bring about and the cultural and human costs of the illegal antiquities market. Recent decades have seen widescale looting of archaeological sites in places that are known to be sources of antique and medieval manuscripts—places like Egypt, Syria, and Iraq. Thus, when manuscripts appear on the antiquities market with no previously documented history, looted sites are a potential source, and indeed the looting itself may be driven by profits from the sale of manuscripts and other artifacts.

And one factor that makes ancient manuscripts attractive to potential buyers is the prospect that they may be studied by experts. There is thus a possibility that the academic study of unprovenanced manuscripts stimulates the trade in such artifacts and encourages looting. Yet, because the illegal trade in antiquities is generally shrouded in mystery, proving beyond doubt that a manuscript was looted is a relatively rare occurrence. Nevertheless, a growing number of scholars and heritage professionals find it likely that there are connections between the academic study of unprovenanced manuscripts, the collection of unprovenanced manuscripts, and the looting of archaeological sites.

What Are "the Rules"?

For well over a century, many nations have had their own laws regarding the sale and movement of manuscripts and other objects identified as having special cultural or historical significance. You can find a searchable list of such laws at the website of **UNESCO**, the United Nations Educational, Scientific and Cultural Organization. There have also been efforts to come up with multinational agreements to regulate and protect such items (see Box 3.1 for one example).

In spite of the existence of these national laws and earlier international agreements, discussions about legal and ethical concerns in the study of manuscripts and other archaeological

---

BOX 3.1. The 1954 Hague Convention

The 1954 Convention for the Protection of Cultural Property in the Event of Armed Conflict is an international treaty governing the treatment during armed conflict of artifacts classified as culturally or historically significant. Following on the destruction caused by the two world wars, this convention encouraged countries to take steps to preserve both their own culturally significant materials and those of other countries in wartime and during occupation. The convention calls upon countries to, among other things, "undertake to prohibit, prevent and, if necessary, put a stop to any form of theft, pillage or misappropriation of, and any acts of vandalism directed against, cultural property." Thus, national governments are charged with the responsibility to ensure the safety of such objects within their borders and to refrain from endangering the cultural heritage artifacts of other countries. If the manuscripts that you want to study first appeared, or were subject to contested claims to ownership, in a region experiencing a time of armed conflict or occupation, it is useful for you to know this in order to make an informed decision about studying them.

artifacts are almost always in some way oriented to what is known as the UNESCO Convention of 1970 (https://en.unesco.org/fighttrafficking/1970). To address rising concerns about the illegal trafficking of cultural heritage items, UNESCO established an international treaty, the UNESCO Convention on the Means of Prohibiting and Preventing the Illicit Import, Export and Transfer of Ownership of Cultural Property. The treaty is based on the idea of national cultural heritage, the idea that the governments of individual nations have a right and a responsibility to protect items within their borders that are deemed to be culturally significant. Basically, the treaty requires that participating nations help to enforce each other's existing national laws to prevent the unauthorized movement of cultural heritage items across international borders.

The treaty went into effect in 1972, so it is usually either the year 1970 or the year 1972 that functions as a shorthand reference to the time when there was wide international acknowledgment that the unregulated trade in antiquities and other culturally important items was problematic. Many academic societies express their ethics policies connected to publication of manuscripts and other artifacts with reference to these years (see Box 3.2 for several examples).

For instance, the Society for Classical Studies provides a detailed statement about the publication of inscribed antiquities with reference to the UNESCO convention. The statement begins by describing the importance of antiquities:

> Artifacts of all sorts, and particularly objects bearing texts, such as inscriptions, papyri, and coins, play central roles in our studies. Questions about their provenance and history can arise in many areas of scholarly work, including first publications of objects and texts and the management of institu-

> **BOX 3.2. Sample Ethics Statements from Academic Societies**
>
> American Society of Overseas Research (ASOR): Policy on Professional Conduct (last updated 2019; https://www.asor.org/about-asor/policies/policy-on-professional-conduct/).
> American Society of Papyrologists (ASP): Resolutions on the Papyrus Trade (2007 and 2021; https://www.papyrology.org/resolutions.html).
> Society for Classical Studies (SCS): Statement on Professional Ethics (last updated 2019; https://classicalstudies.org/about/scs-statement-professional-ethics).
> Society of Biblical Literature (SBL): Policy on Scholarly Presentation and Publication of Ancient Artifacts (last updated 2017; https://www.sbl-site.org/assets/pdfs/SBL-Artifacts-Policy_20160903.pdf).

tional collections. Moreover, the study of the histories of objects has much to contribute to Classical Studies, especially in understanding the full context of the creation and use of objects, and in reception history. Accordingly, members should always be aware of the impact that their professional practice will have on the creation and preservation of information about ancient objects and should exercise due diligence by thoroughly studying the history of the object(s) under study.

It continues with a list of activities to avoid:

In all cases, members should avoid activity that contributes directly or indirectly to the illegal handling of antiquities. In particular, members

> should avoid activity that increases the commercial value of illegally exported objects or which can, even indirectly, lead to further looting.

It invokes the UNESCO convention as "an essential point of reference for avoiding involvement with insufficiently documented antiquities" but reminds members that nations have their own laws as well:

> It is these laws that define objects as stolen and make their possession subject to prosecution. Even objects legally exported well before 1970 can benefit from the investigation of provenance. It is also incumbent upon members to be transparent in all publications about the sources and collection histories of all objects they work with and publish.[1]

Many other academic societies, and also many scholarly journals and publishing houses, take these matters seriously and expect scholars who work on manuscripts to be aware of these concerns. Not everyone, however, is convinced that these kinds of policies are the best way to proceed. Some scholars view studying and publishing manuscripts as both an absolute right and a duty. Others point out that matters are not as black and white as references to the year 1970 can sometimes appear. Many countries did not officially accept the UNESCO convention until decades after it first went into effect; for example, the United States accepted it in 1983, Japan in 1992, South Africa in 1997, the United Kingdom in 2002, and Norway in 2007. Each national government may have different ideas about enforcement of these rules based on when the convention was actually accepted.

Still others challenge the whole idea of a "national cultural heritage" and the notion that national governments should be able to make laws to curb the trade in artifacts. James Cuno, president of the J. Paul Getty Trust from 2011 to 2022, has argued strongly against the philosophy underlying the UNESCO convention:

> All cultures are dynamic, mongrel creations, interrelated such that we all have a stake in their preservation. National retentionist cultural property laws deny this basic truth. They depend on the myth of pure, static, distinct, national cultures. And not just about living cultures, but about ancient cultures, too. They define and seek to regulate access to ancient cultures on the grounds that they belong to the modern nation as the work of its descendents and the origins of its modern culture and identity. They promote a sectarian view of culture and encourage the politics of identity at a time when nationalism and sectarian violence are resurgent around the world.[2]

Those on the other side of the debate often agree that the idea of national cultural heritage is a construction, but they emphasize that the constructed nature of identity is unavoidable and that ancient artifacts often have an important function in local communities. The archaeologist Monica Hanna has argued that "objects also have a role to play in cultural heritage preservation, which has a very clear impact on the consolidation of the identity of living peoples and their archaeological spaces.... The loss of historical objects thus creates a gap in the production of culture in the present."[3]

74 Provenance and Why It Matters

Wading into these heated arguments can be intimidating, but if you carry out due diligence by making a reasonable and good faith effort to discover as much as you can about the history of the manuscript you are studying, you will be able to make an informed decision about the best way to proceed. We cannot tell you how to make these decisions, but we can and do advise you to act in accordance with your professional society's rules and ethical standards. The rest of this chapter will offer some guidance on the steps you can take to think through problems of provenance.

Repositories of Manuscripts

Before you can answer the question "How did this manuscript get here?" it is important to know something about where exactly "here" is. Manuscripts can be found in several different kinds of collections. For heuristic purposes, we distinguish public, private, and heritage collections:

Public collections: collections that are publicly owned and (usually) open to the public. They can be large, such as national museums or libraries. They can be midsize collections, for example, at university libraries. Public collections may also be small and specialized.

Private collections: collections of manuscripts owned and controlled by private actors (companies or individuals). Private collections are most often dependent on market acquisition of manuscripts. The collections vary in both size and level of accessibility to the public.

Heritage collections: holdings of manuscripts that have been kept for generations by groups and communities that identify with the producers or are the historical users and stewards of the manuscripts. Examples of such collections are family-owned manuscript collections in the Middle East, collections that are still in monastic keeping around the world, and groups of manuscripts kept in or in connection with churches, synagogues, mosques, and other places of worship. Most commonly, these collections of manuscripts are privately owned. Accessibility varies.

This typology of collections does not account equally well for all manuscript collections in the world, and the divide is not always as clear-cut as the typology may suggest. For example, many collections began as the private holdings of wealthy individuals but were later acquired by public institutions, such as the library of the 26th Earl of Crawford, James Ludovic Lindsay, whose collection of papyri now forms the nucleus of the papyrus collection at the Rylands Library at the University of Manchester. The Chester Beatty in Dublin is another example. Like many other public collections, this collection began as a private library, in this case the library of Alfred Chester Beatty, an owner of diamond mines in Sierra Leone and copper mines in Northern Rhodesia (modern Zambia). Despite the weaknesses of our typology, we choose to use it here because it matters to our current discussion of legality and ethics. In Chapters 4 and 5, too, the typology is relevant to issues of access, forms of communication with curators, and the practicalities of your work in the reading room.

When you consider visiting a collection of any of the three types, gather information about the status of the collection and its acquisition record. Both public collections and private collections have a mixed record when it comes to the legality of how they obtained their manuscripts. Some public collections and some private collections generally respect international treaties and avoid purchasing manuscripts with insecure provenance. Other collections are less scrupulous about following those guidelines.

Private collections have been subject to considerable scrutiny in recent years. Today, manuscript and textual scholars are divided in their view on private manuscript ownership. Some of your colleagues will, as a matter of principle, never cooperate with private collectors and not work on manuscripts in private collections. These colleagues stress the legal and ethical challenges of working on manuscripts that have been acquired through the antiquities market. They argue that private collectors stimulate the illegal trade of antiquities and that scholars add prestige and authority to the collection and increase the market value of the manuscripts when they publish them or articles about them.

Other colleagues hold the opposite view and defend working with manuscripts in private collections. They maintain that private collectors have saved many manuscripts that otherwise would have been lost or dismantled, and they hold that it is the duty of a scholar to publish any surviving remains of the past.

Yet other colleagues see nuances or add shades of gray. For instance, they may not share in the wholesale condemnation of private collections, but they may tell you that it is more risky to work with a privately owned manuscript because you depend on the goodwill of the collector and because the manuscript you work on may suddenly be sold off without public notice.

You may wonder how we deal with these issues ourselves. Back in 2014, Liv cooperated with a private collector about an exhibit. At that time, she did not see it as problematic. Today, she interprets her cooperation as the result of personal ignorance and the traditional acceptance of working with private

Provenance and Why It Matters

collectors and their holdings in her immediate fields of scholarship. However, in the mid-2010s, the traditional attitudes started to change. Insights that had been developed in neighboring academic fields, such as papyrology and archaeology, increasingly challenged the practices of textual scholars, and the debate grew in intensity—a debate in which Liv argued for caution. In 2015, when a representative of the Green Scholars Initiative—the research unit of what later became the Museum of the Bible in Washington, DC—asked her to work on the Syriac manuscripts in their collection, she turned the offer down.

Currently, Liv acknowledges that deciding whether to study privately held materials, to work in a private collection, may sometimes be complex. For example, due to the tight academic job market, early career scholars may feel that they have no other choice than to take the opportunities that are presented to them. Personally (and with the privilege that a permanent job grants her), she avoids working with privately owned manuscripts because they are often acquired from the antiquities market and their provenance can be problematic or unclear. She does not want to contribute to the academic legitimation of potentially looted or illegally exported goods.

Brent is ambivalent. He and his colleague Daniel Sharp have worked for years at the Fondation Martin Bodmer, an institution that in some ways blurs the line between public and private. It is a private museum and library born from the personal collection of Martin Bodmer (1899–1971), but since 2015 it has been listed in UNESCO's Memory of the World International Register and regularly holds public exhibitions. Brent values his friendships with staff members there and takes pride in his role in digitizing and creating an online catalog of the collection's papyri, which makes images of these important manuscripts freely and widely available for the first time. Yet, in the course of producing the online catalog, Brent and

Daniel experienced friction with the institution on multiple occasions when their requests for access to archival information relating to the purchase of the manuscripts were repeatedly rebuffed. In recent years, changes in both attitudes and staffing have resulted in a more open approach to questions of provenance, which is a promising development, but the whole experience has left Brent with very mixed feelings.

You will have to make up your own mind about these matters. However, especially if you are an early career scholar, we encourage you to tread carefully. Always ask yourself this question: Who stands to gain the most from your work on this manuscript? Whatever your opinions are, given the contested status of private collections, the choice of working on privately held manuscripts may affect your career and your reputation. You must weigh the potential costs and benefits of focusing your efforts on privately held materials.

Although currently it is private collections that are especially contested among many scholars, this does not mean that other types of collections are unproblematic. The acquisition histories of many large public collections in Europe, such as national museums and libraries, are deeply interwoven with the colonial past of the host country. Although the export of a manuscript from its country of origin may have been technically legal and taken place long before the ratification of international conventions, the removal of the manuscript from its previous owners may still raise ethical issues once you start examining the details (Box 3.3). Furthermore, private collectors are not the only ones who may depend on illegal markets. Some public collections have also been formed largely through these markets. The financial history of some collections may also be worth looking into. Who funded the acquisition of the manuscripts, and where did their money come from? The answers to these kinds of questions can be eye-opening.

Provenance and Why It Matters

BOX 3.3. Manuscript Hunting in the Nineteenth Century

In an 1849 book, *Visits to Monasteries in the Levant* (London: John Murray, 1849), 85–88, Robert Curzon (14th Baron Zouche, 1810–1873) provides an example of the colonial logic behind manuscript acquisition. There he describes how he removed manuscripts from the Monastery of the Syrians in the Wadi al-Natrun (Egypt).

> In the morning I went to see the church and all the other wonders of the place, and on making inquiries about the library, was conducted by the old abbot, who was blind, and was constantly accompanied by another monk, into a small upper room in the great square tower, where we found several Coptic manuscripts. Most of these were lying on the floor, but some were placed in niches in the stone wall. They were all on paper, except three or four. One of these was a superb manuscript of the Gospels, with commentaries by the early fathers of the church; two others were doing duty as coverings to a couple of large open pots or jars, which had contained preserves, long since evaporated. I was allowed to purchase these vellum manuscripts, as they were considered to be useless by the monks, principally, I believe, because there were no more preserves in the jars. . . . I had been told, by a French gentleman at Cairo, that there were many ancient manuscripts in the monks' oil cellar; and it was in pursuit of these and the Coptic dictionary that I had undertaken the journey to the Natron Lakes. The abbot positively denied the existence of these books, and we retired from the library to my room with the Coptic manuscripts which they had ceded to me without difficulty. . . . The abbot, his companion, and myself sat down together.

BOX 3.3. *(continued)*

I produced a bottle of rosoglio from my stores, to which I knew that all Oriental monks were partial. . . . Next to the golden key, which masters so many locks, there is no better opener of the heart than a sufficiency of strong drink . . . and talking pleasantly over our bottle till some time passed away, and the face of the blind abbot waxed bland and confiding. . . . I had the great advantage over the good abbot, as I could see the workings of his features and he could not see mine, or note my eagerness about the oil cellar. . . . We then descended a narrow staircase to the oil cellar . . . there were no books here: but taking the candle from the hands of one of the brethren (for they had all wandered in after us, having nothing else to do), I discovered a narrow low door, and, pushing it open, entered into a small closet vaulted with stone which was filled to the depth of two feet or more with the loose leaves of the Syriac manuscripts which now form one of the chief treasures of the British Museum. Here I remained for some time turning over the leaves and digging into the mass of loose vellum pages; by which exertions I raised such a cloud of fine pungent dust that the monks relieved each other in holding our only candle at the door, while the dust made us sneeze incessantly as we turned over the scattered leaves of vellum.

Note how Curzon contrasts the valuable manuscripts with dirt and dust. He suggests that the monks were careless in their interaction with the manuscripts, that they were idle, that they lied, and that they were easy to fool into parting with the manuscripts. He implies that they did not understand the value of these precious items. In Curzon's narrative the manuscripts are essentially begging for the Englishman's intervention.

Provenance and Why It Matters

Life Stories of Manuscripts

Once you have identified the kind of collection where your manuscript resides, it is important to investigate the history of the manuscript itself (Box 3.4). How did it get there? Maybe the manuscript has always resided in the particular monastery and is still a part of the life of a living community. If so, on most occasions the provenance history of the manuscript is reasonably clear.

For libraries and museums, a little more detective work may be necessary. In many collections, the curators have already done some of this research for users. The catalog records for manuscripts, many of which are accessible online, often provide you with a great deal of useful information about provenance. Take, for example, the Austrian National Library's online record for a parchment codex containing a lavishly illustrated copy of *De materia medica* by the Roman physician Dioscorides, Vienna, Cod. Med. gr. 1, the "Vienna Dioscorides" (http://data.onb.ac.at/rec/AC14452244). A section of the entry

---

BOX 3.4. Questions to Ask Yourself about Provenance

- Where did your manuscript originate?
- Where and when did it move / change owners / cross national borders?
- Did it leave its country of origin before or after 1970?
- Did it leave its country of origin before or after that country passed laws about the export of antiquities?
- Did it leave its country of origin or its holding institution during a time of war or occupation?
- Are there gaps in its ownership history?

called "Provenance/History of the Resource" provides a partial chain of ownership:

- Early sixth century CE: Gift to Juliana Anicia (as we know from the dedication page of the codex)
- Owned by the Prodromu Petra Monastery (Constantinople)
- 1405–1406 Restored by Johannes Chortasmenos
- Hamon (private physician to Suleiman II)
- 1576 Purchased through Augerius von Busbeck for the court library under Hugo Blotius

You will, of course, be curious about who these figures are and how exactly these names and dates are known, but this online catalog entry provides a good starting point for provenance research.

Not every catalog entry will be so straightforward. In fact, almost none will. In some cases, you may find an abbreviated reference for an acquisition ("1971a," or something like that) in which case there is likely a separate page that has a list of acquisitions by date that provides further details. On other occasions, online repository records might fail to provide you with any provenance details. The next step is to see if there is a print catalog that deals with the acquisition of your manuscript. Further investigation into archives on-site can be part of your research trip if you have the time and resources to explore some of your unanswered questions (see Chapter 4).

On occasion these institutional sources can get you only so far. For instance, you may be able to find the name of an auction house (like Christie's or Sotheby's) and a date in the 1990s but nothing more. In this case, you can turn to auction catalogs, which are available in some research libraries. You can also contact research staff at auction houses. They can

Provenance and Why It Matters

sometimes be very helpful and have access to records that are otherwise unavailable. But be prepared for some frustration, for auction houses often operate under various kinds of non-disclosure agreements and sometimes have a vested interest in obscuring the histories of artifacts in order to protect themselves from bad publicity and potential legal troubles.

If, at the end of the day, you are truly stumped, you can also go back to the repository website and find the contact information for the responsible curator and ask about the provenance of the manuscript. Let the curator know what research you have already done. And always be polite. Some institutions can be sensitive about issues of provenance, so use your discretion.

To Study or Not to Study?

Hopefully, at the end of your research you have found good evidence that your manuscript has a documented chain of ownership going back at least as early as 1970. If so, you have cleared the bar for most academic societies that offer guidelines for studying and publishing manuscripts. But what happens if the best you can do is trace the ownership history of your manuscript back to the 1980s or 1990s or to a vague and unverifiable claim of provenance: "a Swiss dealer in the 1960s" or "part of an old family collection from the nineteenth century"? Or what if you strongly suspect that your manuscript has been looted, stolen, or smuggled illegally? In these cases, you have a decision to make. Depending on the academic community with which you identify, there may be a set of guidelines you can consult for advice about how to proceed (see Box 3.2).

In addition to being aware of your discipline's ethics policies, you should also give some thought to potential legal ramifications of continuing to work on such materials. Patty Gerstenblith, a specialist in cultural heritage law, has offered this advice:

> If a scholar is aware of the illegal nature of the artifacts he or she handles or engages in conscious avoidance of the relevant facts, the scholar is as guilty of breaking the law as the looters, sellers, smugglers and purchasers who traffic in such objects—in fact, it is very much the scholar's business to avoid handling stolen or otherwise illegal artifacts. . . . So long as there are scholars willing to authenticate and publish such artifacts and so long as scholars continue to evade the reach of the law despite their handling of stolen property, scholars will continue to confer value, and the illegal trade will continue while the world and the countries of origin suffer the consequences of loss of knowledge about the past.[4]

Some scholars contest views like Gerstenblith's and appeal to norms and values they regard as having higher validity than laws passed by national legislatures and treaties ratified by national governments. John Boardman, the former Lincoln Professor of Classical Archaeology and Art at Oxford University, has formulated this position: "What can be made of a law that regards objects with no apparent pedigree, or rather those who handle and study them, to be guilty until proved innocent? This is not natural justice. Objects cannot be 'tainted' or 'illicit,' but only be so described by scholars who do not understand them, or by legislators. Objects are testaments of antiquity, whether handled by a thief or scholar; their integrity must be respected and their safety assured."[5]

Provenance and Why It Matters

Whichever of these arguments you ultimately find persuasive, it is important that you give these matters serious thought. After carrying out your provenance research, you may decide that undertaking further study of the manuscript in question is not worth the trouble and instead keep open to the possibility of working with a different manuscript. Or, more positively, you may find that your provenance research was itself interesting enough to publish.

The bottom line is that if you find yourself confronted with a manuscript that has an inadequate provenance history, you must make a choice. Or, rather, you have the privilege of making a choice. Not everyone is fortunate enough to be able to travel to a collection and study a manuscript. Also, scholars from countries (like Egypt and Syria) that are the sources of the manuscripts are often the ones who face special challenges in visiting distant collections: financial needs, visa restrictions, and the like. So keep in mind that the decision to study or not to study an unprovenanced manuscript is about more than just your intellectual curiosity or a line on your CV. Rather, as the archaeologist and cultural historian Akinwumi Ogundiran has noted, "It is about the power to do, act, rationalize, and justify what we think is appropriate. It is important that we recognize that not everyone has this kind of power. The pursuit of knowledge is intimately connected to the global dynamics of social, economic, and political inequality."[6]

Manuscripts are artifacts that have histories. Learning as much as you can about the history of your manuscript can allow you to see how the manuscript has intersected with the lives of other people, how it has affected other people in the past, and how it may continue to affect people today. If you study and publish something about a manuscript, you become part of its story. Make sure it is a story that you are comfortable telling.

Further Reading

GENERAL DEBATES ON CULTURAL HERITAGE

Boardman, John. "Archaeologists, Collectors, and Museums." In *Whose Culture? The Promise of Museums and the Debate over Antiquities,* ed. James Cuno, 107–124. Princeton: Princeton University Press, 2012.

Cuno, James. *Who Owns Antiquity? Museums and the Battle over Our Cultural Heritage.* Princeton: Princeton University Press, 2008.

Hanna, Monica. "Cultural Heritage Attrition in Egypt." In *Testing the Canon of Ancient Near Eastern Art and Archaeology,* ed. Amy Rebecca Gansell and Ann Shafer, 315–318. Oxford: Oxford University Press, 2020.

Mbembe, Achille. *Out of the Dark Night: Essays on Decolonization.* New York: Columbia University Press, 2021.

Renfrew, Colin. *Loot, Legitimacy, and Ownership: The Ethical Crisis in Archaeology.* London: Duckworth, 2000.

COLLECTION HISTORIES

Cuéllar, Gregory L. *Empire, the British Museum, and the Making of the Biblical Scholar in the Nineteenth Century.* London: Palgrave Macmillan, 2019.

Gerstenblith, Patty. "Hobby Lobby, the Museum of the Bible, and the Law." In *Antiquities Smuggling in the Real and Virtual World,* ed. Layla Hashemi and Louise Shelley, 59–95. New York: Routledge, 2022.

Haug, Brendan. "Politics, Partage, and Papyri: Excavated Texts between Cairo and Ann Arbor (1924–1953)." *American Journal of Archaeology* 125 (2021): 143–163. Open access: https://doi.org/10.3764/aja.125.1.0143.

Lin, Yii-Jan. "Reading across the Archives: Mining the Beatty Narrative." In *The Chester Beatty Biblical Papyri at Ninety,* ed. Garrick V. Allen, Usama Gad, Kelsie G. Rodenbiker, and Jill Unkel, 83–96. Berlin: De Gruyter, 2023. Open access: https://doi.org/10.1515/9783110781304-006.

Nongbri, Brent. *God's Library: The Archaeology of the Earliest Christian Manuscripts.* New Haven: Yale University Press, 2018.

LEGACIES OF COLONIALISM

Curzon, Robert. *Visits to Monasteries in the Levant.* London: John Murray, 1849. https://archive.org/details/visitstomon asteroocurz/page/n7/mode/2up.

El Houkayem, Maroun. "Orientalism, Disorientation, and the 'Other Side of the World.'" *Studies in Late Antiquity* 7 (2023): 171–183.

Smith, Claire. "Visa Stories: Human Rights, Structural Violence, and Ethical Globalisation." *Archaeologies* 3 (2007): 179–185. This article introduces a set of essays on the challenges that some archaeologists have faced in trying to obtain and use visas, especially visas to the United States and the United Kingdom.

ACADEMICS AND THE ETHICS OF PUBLICATION

Brodie, Neil. "Congenial Bedfellows? The Academy and the Antiquities Trade." *Journal of Contemporary Criminal Justice* 27 (2011): 411–440.

Brodie, Neil. "Scholarly Engagement with Collections of Unprovenanced Ancient Texts." In *Cultural Heritage at Risk,* ed. Kurt Almqvist and Louise Belfrage, 123–142. Stockholm: Ax:son Johnson Foundation, 2016.

Justnes, Årstein. "Fake Fragments, Flexible Provenances: Eight Aramaic 'Dead Sea Scrolls' from the 21st Century." In *Vision, Narrative, and Wisdom in the Aramaic Texts from Qumran,* ed. Mette Bundvad and Kasper Siegesmund, 242–272. Studies on the Texts of the Desert of Judah 131. Leiden: Brill, 2019. Open access: https://doi.org/10.1163/9789004413733_014.

Kersel, Morag M. "To Publish or Not to Publish? This Is No Longer the Question." *Bryn Mawr Classical Review,* Feb. 5, 2023. Open access: https://bmcr.brynmawr.edu/2023/2023.02.05/.

Kersel, Morag M. "Do the Right Thing." *Levant* 55 (2023): 255–261. Open access: https://www.tandfonline.com/doi/full/10.1080/00758914.2023.2274666?src=recsys.

Lied, Liv Ingeborg. "Someone Else's Manuscripts: The Ethics of Textual Scholarship." In *Variant Scholarship: Ancient Texts in Modern Contexts,* ed. Neil Brodie, Morag M. Kersel, and Josephine Munch Rasmussen, 189–201. Leiden: Sidestone Press, 2023.

Nongbri, Brent. "The Ethics of Publication: Papyrology." *Bryn Mawr Classical Review,* May 25, 2022. Open access: https://bmcr.brynmawr.edu/2022/2022.05.25/.

Ogundiran, Akinwumi. "The License of Power in African Art." *African Arts* 53 (2020): 18–19. This article is one of several collected in this issue of *African Arts* under the title "Knowledge, Ethics, and Power: Publishing African Objects without Clear African Provenance."

Rasmussen, Josephine Munch, and Christopher Prescott. "Exploring the 'Cozy Cabal of Academics, Dealers and Collectors' through the Schøyen Collection." *Heritage—Open Access Journal of Knowledge, Conservation and Management of Cultural and Natural Heritage* 3 (2020): 68–91.

Sabar, Ariel. *Veritas: A Harvard Professor, a Con Man, and the Gospel of Jesus's Wife.* New York: Doubleday, 2020.

4

Getting Access and Planning Your Stay

In Chapters 2 and 3, we guided you through the process of finding your manuscript and learning about its provenance. If you have determined that you need to see this manuscript in person, this chapter will help you maximize your chances of getting access to the collection and help you plan your visit. There is no single recipe for accessing manuscript collections. Each collection has its own policies and procedures. This chapter will let you know what to expect in some scenarios.

Planning a visit is a key aspect of manuscript study. Important practicalities include: how to begin the process of accessing a manuscript, how to contact curators, how to budget time and money for your stay, and what not to forget on your trip. We also address some of the challenges of accessing manuscripts and some of the ethically fraught issues that you may encounter on the way. Getting access sometimes depends on your status, affiliation, or connections. Every so often, your economic resources, the political situation, and your ethnicity or gender may play a role as well. Finally, we discuss how

Digital Images or Autoptic Study?

In our view, having at least some experience with manuscripts is an essential part of the competence of any textual scholar. For many research projects, being familiar with the immediate material context of the texts you are working on is vital. Indeed, for some projects, exploring the relationship between the text and the manuscript is the project itself. However, before you start the process of getting access to a manuscript, you should ask yourself whether your project requires you to work autoptically on it. Maybe you don't need to observe the manuscript itself; maybe consulting digital images of the manuscript will suffice.

During the past two decades, many large manuscript collections have been digitized. More and more manuscripts are now available in the form of digital images online. Several digital repositories, such as HMML, provide you with excellent visual access to manuscript images. The digitization of manuscripts has in many ways revolutionized manuscript research. It provides easy access to images of manuscripts. You do not even have to leave your desk: the images are available at your fingertips.

If you are lucky, your manuscript belongs to one of the collections that has been digitized, and you will find it online (Box 4.1). Some of the recent digitization projects offer high-quality outputs. Those responsible for the digitizing knew the needs of both textual scholars and those interested in manuscripts as cultural artifacts and imaged the manuscripts to meet their needs. In these cases, digital images may provide unrivaled visual access. Not only is the text in the columns easy to read on the screen, but users can zoom in on details in

BOX 4.1. Some Major Collections of Digital Images of Manuscripts

There are many online repositories with digital images of manuscripts. This is a small selection of some of the more important collections.

- Digital Bodleian (https://digital.bodleian.ox.ac.uk/) provides access to many of the medieval manuscripts housed in Oxford's Bodleian Library.
- DigiVatLib (https://digi.vatlib.it/) is the online repository of the Vatican Library, containing images of many manuscripts in the Vatican Library's collections.
- e-codices (https://www.e-codices.unifr.ch/en), the Virtual Manuscript Library of Switzerland, provides images of medieval manuscripts from many collections in Switzerland.
- Gallica (https://gallica.bnf.fr) contains digital versions, both new images and digitized microfilms, of many manuscripts in the Bibliothèque nationale de France and other French collections.
- Hill Museum and Manuscript Library (https://hmml .org/) hosts images of manuscripts from a wide variety of traditions and locations, including the 60,000-plus images of the Vööbus Syriac Manuscript Collection.
- Library of Congress (https://www.loc.gov/) preserves scans of microfilm images of manuscripts from many monastic collections, including the large collections from the monasteries of Mount Athos.

Another major collection of digital images of manuscripts is hosted by the British Library, but at the time of writing, these images remain inaccessible after a cyberattack on the library in 2023. This is an important reminder of the vulnerability of the digital mediation of cultural heritage.

the margins and zoom out to see the entirety of each artifact. At its best, digital imaging of manuscripts remedies some of the former elitism of Manuscript Studies, providing more democratic access and access from afar.

For many projects, consulting digital images may suffice. Getting access to a manuscript may be time-consuming, traveling to the collection may be expensive, and air travel leaves a large carbon footprint. Furthermore, some manuscripts are fragile and will not survive heavy handling. Curators may restrict access to these manuscripts to protect them from further wear and tear—including the wear and tear that your hands would cause.

Yet on many occasions working on digital images may not be the best option for you. In the first instance, you may want to work on a manuscript that has not been digitized. This is still the case for the bulk of all manuscripts, and this challenge is unfortunately particularly palpable for those of us who work on literatures that are considered outside the main cultural or religious canons. Also, the quality of the digital remediation of manuscripts varies considerably, and the images may not give you the information you need. The older the digital images are, the more frequently their usability is a problem. For example, the images may include only one face of a papyrus fragment, or the images may lack a scale. Some images are in grayscale and render ink colors, textures of the writing surface, and traces of active readers hard or impossible to see. Images of large tomes may leave out the margins or cut right across additional notes. Some features, such as folds and cuts, may be difficult to see on the computer screen, even in good digital photos. What letters are hiding in the barely visible gutter of that bifolium? Are you looking at a photo of the actual bifolium, or has someone artificially connected images of two single folia side by side (see Figure 1.10)?

Getting Access and Planning Your Stay

Furthermore, your project may demand more than the access that the computer interface offers you. If your research includes questions about the historical handling of certain manuscripts, for example, you may need to know what the manuscripts smell like (incense? mold?) or how heavy or bulky they are. If this is the case, digital images of manuscripts can't replace in-person engagement with the physical artifacts, and you should try to get access to the real thing.

Getting Access

If you plan to visit a large public collection, the obvious place to start is with information available online, such as guidelines at library or collection websites. Most often, you will find the information you need there, including descriptions of access procedures and the relevant contact information. For example, if your manuscript is kept at the British Library or in the Vatican Library, their websites provide all the necessary information. Read carefully and follow the directions.

Some collections, such as those at the Chester Beatty, have made the access procedure all-digital. To gain access to many other collections, however, you have to send a curator an email. Formulate a polite, informative, and brief email (Box 4.2). Once you have submitted your request, wait for the curator to be in touch with you. Be patient: Curators in large collections receive many inquiries similar to yours. You cannot expect an answer the next day.

For smaller public collections, less research-intensive libraries, and for some large but less public-facing manuscript collections, access information may not be as easily available. Try to find the contact information of a curator or an academic librarian on the website. If this is not available, any contact information at the website may give you a first lead. Sometimes

BOX 4.2. Sample Email to a Curator

Dear Dr. Conservesitall,

I hope this email finds you well. I am part of a research project that aims to explore all surviving pandects (full-Bible manuscripts) in Latin, Greek, and Syriac, and I have been assigned the task of studying the Syriac pandects. At the time of writing, I have explored all the surviving pre-13th-century pandects with the exception of X, which is kept at your institution. It would be a great help for my research to be allowed to access this manuscript.

Kind regards,

Liv Ingeborg Lied

---

getting access to these types of collections involves figuring out the social hierarchies and division of labor at the institution. These are not always easily conceivable or logical to an outsider. The answer to your first email may therefore be an instruction to contact someone else, which may send you in a loop. Do not give up until your email lands in the computer of the person who can actually help you.

If your manuscript is kept in a heritage collection, try contacting the head of the collection if that information is available. Sometimes that one contact is all it takes. If not, think of someone in your field who may help you get in touch. Email a colleague who gained access earlier and ask for advice. You can also make an appeal to the social media hivemind: ask the networked scholarly community in a Facebook group or pose a question in an academic email list catering to scholars

Getting Access and Planning Your Stay

in your field. Some lists, such as the Hugoye list and the PAPY list, are generous environments in which scholars across the world pose questions, share experiences, and offer their assistance to colleagues.

We do not discuss private collections here (see Chapter 3). There are ethical and legal challenges, and there are risks. Also, private collectors have their own sets of rules for working with their collections, so offering generally applicable and effective advice is not really possible.

Roadblocks and Reflections

Our experience is that the staff at libraries and museums will go to great lengths to help scholars. Still, at times they may have good reasons for denying access. On a few occasions, the situation may be complex.

Many collections will not accept you unless you present a letter of recommendation (Box 4.3). The letter writer must be someone who carries a certain authority, preferably, a scholar with a standing in the field or someone that the staff at the collection already knows. Your thesis supervisor or the dean at your institution may also write such a letter for you. When you request a letter of recommendation, be sure to provide your letter writer with detailed information about your project as well as practical information, such as the date by which you need the letter sent. Also remember that asking a colleague for a letter of recommendation comes with some responsibility on your part. You do not want to risk jeopardizing your colleague's relationship with the collection. Ask someone who knows you and your work. For students, the best choice may be your supervisor. Remember to say thank you to that colleague. Always.

Sometimes the authorities at collections are hesitant to allow you access even if you provide a letter of recommendation.

> ### BOX 4.3. Sample Letter of Recommendation
>
> To the Admissions Office,
>
> This letter will introduce Ms. Ima Newatthis, a doctoral researcher at Manuscript University. I have known her since 2015, when she was a MPhil student at the same institution. Ms. Newatthis is writing a PhD thesis on the modern history of several manuscripts now held in your collection, and her research will be considerably improved if she can access the following items at your collection: [. . .]. Ms. Newatthis is a very promising early-career scholar, and she can be trusted to make proper use of materials in the collection. I hope you will provide her with access to the resources that she requests.
>
> If you need any further information from me, I can be reached via email.
>
> Thank you very much for your consideration.
>
> Sincerely,
>
> Brent Nongbri

Some heritage collections, in particular, may be reluctant to let you in. There may be good reasons for their reluctance. The long history of European acquisition of manuscripts from Africa and the Middle East may give you one indication as to why heritage collections such as monastic libraries will not necessarily accept someone they do not know. Since the sixteenth century, European scholars, manuscript hunters, and others have visited monasteries in these areas and asked to see manuscripts. Some left carrying irreplaceable items, and the

Getting Access and Planning Your Stay

nature of their transactions was seldom in the monasteries' favor. Given this unfortunate prehistory, those who are now the guardians of the manuscripts may have the best of reasons for being skeptical about your request.

Authorities at public collections may also be hesitant. Sometimes they have good reasons for denying access to a particular manuscript. You could receive a "no" because the manuscript is undergoing conservation work at the moment or because no one will ever be allowed access to this particular manuscript due to its fragile condition. Or you might learn that a given repository may have a blanket rule disallowing any in-person consultation of manuscripts that have been digitized. These factors are beyond your control. Remember that working on manuscripts is not a right. Your needs are not the only needs—the well-being of the manuscripts trumps them. Also understand that not every collection has the necessary resources to host scholars. An ignored or denied request can be the result of overworked and underpaid staff or lack of essential equipment.

On other occasions, the decision not to grant access to a manuscript may be ungrounded and unfair. Access is not always equally distributed. Some scholars gain access with ease, others have to fight for it, and some never get access to the manuscripts they want to see. The "no" may be the result of how curators have perceived you, your status, and your experience. Prejudice may be involved. If you are a woman or a person of color, or young (according to academic standards), carry a passport from a country outside Europe and the United States, or have some combination of these characteristics, you should not necessarily *expect* to be treated badly, but you should bear in mind that in some collections you may not be served according to the same standards as some of your other colleagues are.

If you know that other scholars have recently accessed the manuscript you want to consult, or if you have a hunch that you have been treated unfairly, you may try to influence the decision. Liv has done this with success on a couple of occasions. Back in the 2010s, she was once denied access to a manuscript in a large university collection. She suspected that her age, gender, nationality, and/or affiliation had not worked in her favor—they did not serve as traditional markers of authority. Her hypothesis was that the person representing the collection had not perceived her as a professional player. She sent a new email in which she highlighted her own authority, competence, and experience: "I am a full professor"; "I have worked in the X, Y and Z collections," "I have studied all the other manuscripts of this kind—this one is the only one I am missing." It worked. At other times patience pays off. If you can shift your work schedule to put off a visit for a few months, or even a year or more, a turnover in staffing can work to your advantage. (Of course, the opposite is also true!) Brent was long denied access to a library, but a change in the staff led to an immediate change in openness, and he was welcomed to the collection.

Sometimes you will have to accept that you will not get access to the manuscript you want to see. Some monasteries exclude women from their premises and thus exclude women scholars from the manuscript collection. The leadership or staff at some manuscript collections may also be engaged in power struggles or stuck in privilege structures that exclude large numbers of potential readers. Although many of these circumstances are unfair and problematic, you will need to choose your battles carefully. And you may not win.

Planning Your Stay

Your access has been granted. Congratulations! It is time to start planning your stay.

Getting Access and Planning Your Stay

An important part of the initial correspondence with the curator or other representative of the collection is agreeing on a timeframe for your stay. Your visit may cause additional work on their part, and they need to know when to expect you. For example, they need to figure out whether the manuscript you are interested in is available, whether there is desk space, and whether the necessary staff will be free to assist you. For you, setting the date of your stay means that you can now get down to planning the details of your visit.

BUDGETING WITH TIME AND MONEY

After you have agreed with the institution about the general date of your visit, the next step is budgeting with time and money. How much time do you have available, and how much time do you need to fulfill the purpose of your stay? Often these two concerns are in conflict, and you will have to bargain with yourself. On the one hand, you may have a family or others who are dependent on you, or you may have work commitments that affect the length of your stay. On the other hand, you do need a certain amount of time with the manuscript to get the job done.

Calculating how much time you will need with a manuscript is hard. Liv has spent weeks on some manuscripts but only hours on others. Of course, the time you will need with a manuscript depends on your research project and your experience with manuscript work. If your aim is to check one specific textual variant, one marginal note, or a correction in a manuscript you know already relatively well—for instance, from digital images—an afternoon may be enough. If you plan to map and understand the codicological features and page layout of a manuscript, you may need several days. If you are tracing the work of a particular copyist, corrector, or note writer across several manuscripts, or if you are interested in finding traces of use by active readers, block out a week in your calendar. If you are new to manuscript study and planning your first visit, keep in mind that literally *everything* takes time: maneuvering and grasping the design of the physical artifact, understanding the layout of the page, and even reading the letters of the text. The text on the manuscript page does not look like text on a page of a critical edition. Give yourself space to learn.

Even with increasing experience, you may find budgeting time demanding. One reason is that you do not always know what you will find in a manuscript. You may come to the collection with clear ideas in mind, but very often the manuscript has other plans for you! Even when you think that you know it from descriptions that others have made—for instance, in critical editions—the manuscript may offer you surprises that change everything you thought and planned. Such discoveries are part of the excitement of working with manuscripts and also the reason why autoptic inspection is so important, but as a consequence, planning a stay is notoriously difficult.

Additional challenges to planning are the procedures and routines of the collection you plan to visit. If you are heading to a monastery, your work may be limited to a few hours per day. Other collections may have unexpected opening hours. The reading room at the Bibliothèque nationale de France opens at 10:00 a.m. (2:00 p.m. on Mondays). To those of us who are early risers, that seems late in the day. Other collections may close earlier than you expect or offer generous siesta time in the middle of the day. Sometimes your work gets delayed because of practical complications or administrative routines. Some collections have set hours for ordering manuscripts, or it may take time to get the manuscript up to you (it tends to be "up") from the archives, or maybe you ordered the wrong manuscript and must repeat the entire procedure, or another reader may be working on your manuscript (make sure to befriend that person!).

Getting Access and Planning Your Stay

Our best advice is to be realistic about what you can accomplish in the time you actually have. Do not expect to cover everything you originally planned to. You may need to visit the collection more than once.

Working with manuscripts also means budgeting with money. How much money do you have available? How can you cover subsistence and travel costs on a budget? Because of the colonial history that came to decide the current locations of archives, thousands of manuscripts are held in collections in European and US cities. These cities are often high-cost environments.

Financial and time costs unfortunately mean that going to a collection to work on manuscripts is not equally available for all. The inequity is obvious and reflects the history of Manuscript Studies: for a long time, studying manuscripts was an elite occupation. Historically, readers had to have the money—and the time—to visit the places where manuscripts were held. This is still the case. Cost levels vary from town to town, but the daily spending in high-cost cities like Paris, Munich, Geneva, and London is hard to push below €100–150. In major US cities you must prepare to spend $150–200. Do you have travel money as part of your position? Are there stipends you can apply for? Maybe you can combine visits to collections with other business, such as going to funded conferences, or arrange a funded speaking engagement in the town you are visiting.

WHERE TO STAY, HOW TO GET THERE,
AND WHERE TO EAT

Make sure that you choose a hotel/bed-and-breakfast/hostel/rental that is located in a safe area. You may end up working late hours and walking back to your room after dark. Preferably, the place is close to the collection. That diminishes the need for long late-evening walks. You may also want to go back to your room and take a quick nap during the day, since manuscript work can be exhausting. Staying nearby can be a blessing. Ask around! Ask friends in your online networks and colleagues in your workplace if they have any recommendations.

Being permanently employed in an academic institution in a high-cost country, we acknowledge that we are in a privileged situation. Nonetheless, we have been traveling on tight budgets for years, and quite often we still do. Brent may stay with friends to cut costs (and enjoy good company) while conducting research at university collections. In expensive cities, he often casts the net beyond typical hotels and has stayed in budget accommodations run by, for instance, the Salvation Army.

If you are on a budget, buy a ticket to the train, bus, or plane well in advance of your travel date. Often the cheapest tickets sell out first. If you are working at a large public museum or library, there may be an affordable, in-house lunch offering. If not, follow the trail of employees and other readers at lunchtime. They tend to know the good, inexpensive places to eat. Alternatively, try out food trucks, pizzerias, and lunch-of-the-day offers at nearby restaurants.

WHAT TO BRING

Before you leave home, make absolutely sure that you carry the essentials. To do your work properly, you need your laptop or tablet—alternatively a decent notebook and pencils. If you have PDF files of editions or articles related to your manuscript that you might want to consult when you have the manuscript in front of you, make sure you have those on your laptop and not an external drive or in the cloud: you can't always count on wireless being available at a collection. Carry a dictionary, digital or book format, if you need one.

Getting Access and Planning Your Stay

If you will be permitted to take your own photos in the reading room, bring your camera, or bring your mobile phone if its camera is good enough to produce high-resolution images. If the images are only meant for your personal use to aid in your research process, and as long as you are in fact able to see details clearly in the images, you do not have to worry about image resolution. However, if the plan is to use the images in a future publication, the recommended resolution is 300 **DPI** or more. DPI means "dots per inch." The higher the DPI, the sharper the image. Anything below 150 DPI is a low-resolution image, and most publishers will not accept it for publication. If your phone or camera has geolocation services, you may want to make sure they are activated so that your photos are geotagged.

For some visits, both Liv and Brent have brought a Dino-Lite microscope. It is a travel-sized handheld digital microscope that enables you to magnify and sharpen details. It can connect to your laptop, either by USB port or wirelessly, and some models can take digital images with infrared and ultraviolet illumination. Prices vary, but these microscopes can be expensive. Ask your institution if they would be interested in buying one for you now and for the benefit of all staff with similar interests. If you plan on bringing one, be sure to ask the curator for permission to use it well in advance of your arrival date.

Make sure to bring a ruler. You will need it. We recommend a clear plastic ruler, which most collections will allow; metal rulers or even wooden rulers with a metal edge are forbidden in many collections. Some scholars also bring a magnifying glass. Some wear a face mask when working on manuscripts. Bring one if you think it protects the manuscripts—and yourself and your fellow readers. Pack formal but comfy clothing: combine formal-enough-to-be-taken-seriously with comfortable-enough-to-make-sitting-all-day-bearable. Dressing in layers can be helpful, for reading rooms can be kept at quite cool temperatures all year round. You may also opt for running or walking gear for leisure time and a good fiction book or your favorite streaming device for lonely evenings.

The most important formal document to bring with you is your passport or ID card. The large majority of collections will ask for proof of identity. If you are not a citizen of the country you visit, they will almost certainly ask to see your passport. Apart from the passport, different collections require different types of documentation. Some collections state explicitly at their website what they need from you—make sure to read the requirements carefully well in advance of your trip. The British Library, for example, requires proof of residency. Depending on how fast (read: slow) the bureaucracy in your home country works, you will have to order this documentation weeks or even months ahead of your trip.

Other collections have no formal requirements, or at least they do not list any on their websites. Often, however, there are informal, taken-for-granted requirements, which you will have to figure out on your own before you go. This sometimes leaves you in a situation where you have to guess about certain rules, and you can expect eye rolls from the staff if you have guessed incorrectly. Also, you may be called upon to show documentation of your academic status and affiliation (a business card or the like), a letter of recommendation, or a document that sketches out some plans for your stay at the collection. Again, ask an experienced colleague or your favorite digital hivemind what to expect at any particular collection.

Some travelers need a visa to be allowed into the country: the inequity of academic work possibilities shows up again. Traveling to European or US cities, which hold so many of the manuscript collections, is not equally possible for all. Some scholars do not get a visa and consequently cannot go.

Before you go, be sure to double-check that the manuscripts you have ordered will indeed be available upon your

Getting Access and Planning Your Stay

arrival. At most collections they are, but you cannot take their availability for granted. Both Liv and Brent have approached the desk in a reading room only to be told that unfortunately the manuscripts they had ordered were not available for inspection after all. Clearly, it would have been better to know that before traveling half the continent to get there (Box 4.4).

BOX 4.4. What to Bring

Musts

- Passport or ID card; visa if required
- Other required documentation
- Computer or pencil and notebook
- Camera or cell phone, if photos are permitted
- Plastic ruler
- Formal yet comfy clothing
- Proper adapters for charging

Maybes, depending on the collection

- Proof of residency
- A letter of recommendation
- Documentation of academic affiliation
- A plan for your stay at the collection

Options

- Microscope or magnifying glass
- Informal clothing; walking or running shoes
- Leisure reading
- A pair of gloves that fit (see Box 5.1)
- A face mask

Access Denied

Your access was denied. What do you do? Once you have come to terms with the disappointment, go for plan B, C, or D.

Plan B: Rally your allies! Does anyone in your network have images of the manuscript that they can share with you? Use your social media network again, or ask your supervisor or a senior colleague to assist you. Very often somebody out there will have images that they are willing to share. Do not underestimate old pictures. You may be in for a surprise. Sometimes old images display the text on a manuscript in a way that is no longer available with the physical artifact itself. Chemical decay is a natural part of the biography of a manuscript, and an old picture preserves an instant in time, a snapshot at an earlier stage of decay. The old capture may in fact make it easier for you to read the text.

Plan C: Make the most of digital images! You already decided that you needed to see the actual manuscript, but if access is denied, take advantage of whatever digitizations are available. If you do choose to work on images, do it with methodological and epistemological finesse. Remember that the digital images offer you visual access but that you cannot feel the texture of the parchment, weigh the codex in your hands, or obtain the same understanding of the artifact that you would if you could use all your senses. Still, working with images is a mode of study in its own right. There is no indexical relationship between image and artifact: the image is not a one-to-one representation of the manuscript. In other words, when you work with images, you are not working on the physical manuscript but a remediation, which has affordances in its own right. When you publish your work, make sure to be transparent about this, and include some reflections of the limits and possibilities involved.

Plan D: Redefine your project! You are not the first, and will not be the last, in the history of the academy who has to rethink a project because of being denied access to essential source materials. Colleagues in the Archaeology Department depend on permission to dig, but permissions are far from always approved. Colleagues in anthropology and other fields that depend on ethnographic methods have often had to change their projects due to sudden warfare or other social unrest. In the early 2020s, the COVID-19 pandemic challenged a whole range of planned research projects across academic fields. Sometimes we are simply unable to study the artifacts we wish to study in the ways that we wish to study them. Curse the gods of manuscript access. Then move on.

Further Reading

Bell, Joshua A., Kimberly Christen, and Mark Turin. "Introduction: After the Return." *Museum Anthropology Review* 7 (2013): 1–21.

Davis, Stephen J. "Manuscripts, Monks, and *Mufattishīn:* Digital Access and Concerns of Cultural Heritage in the Yale Monastic Archaeology Project." In *Digital Biblical Studies: Visualisation and Epistemology,* ed. Claire Clivaz and David Hamidovic, 70–83. Leiden: Brill, 2019.

Lied, Liv Ingeborg. "Digitization and Manuscripts as Visual Objects: Reflections from a Media Studies Perspective." In *Digital Biblical Studies: Visualisation and Epistemology,* ed. Claire Clivaz and David Hamidovic, 15–29. Leiden: Brill, 2019.

Mitchell, William J. T. *Image Science: Iconology, Visual Culture, and Media Aesthetics.* Chicago: University of Chicago Press, 2015.

5

In the Reading Room with Your Manuscript

For most scholars, time spent in the actual presence of manuscripts is limited. When the library staff has brought you a manuscript, the goal is to work attentively, efficiently, and diligently. How do you make the most of your time with the manuscript? This chapter offers advice, ranging from practicalities to power dynamics in the reading room. The stress here will be on your responsibility for the welfare of the manuscript and on ways of looking at it with the eyes of a scholar who is doing more than reading a text.

Arriving at the Collection

If you have an early morning appointment in the reading room, be on time. Curators and library staff do not fancy latecomers and no-shows. They have planned for your arrival, and you should honor your commitment. If you arrived the day before your scheduled visit, you might make a test run. Walking from your lodgings to the collection will teach you the way there and give you a sense of how long getting there actually takes, as opposed to the Google Maps estimate.

In the Reading Room with Your Manuscript 109

Before you close your room door, though, make sure you collect your gear. In the previous chapter, we listed some of the essentials. This is not the time to leave things behind in a drawer.

When you arrive at the collection, step inside. Then pause and observe. If you have arrived at a major public library or museum, you have probably already read about the admission procedures online. Since this is your first time at the collection, you will first head to the Admissions Office to procure a reader's card or other formal evidence of admission. The staff in the Admissions Office will want to see your passport. Sometimes they ask for proof of your residential address. At some collections, they may want to make sure that you actually have the credentials that you say you have or that you have a plan for your visit. Make sure, then, that you have a list of the manuscripts you want to see and why or, alternatively, a list of the things you need to check in the manuscript you are there to review. You may also need proof of your academic affiliation and record, for example, an employee ID card, a business card, or a CV. Remember that it is the staff's job to protect the manuscripts from potentially unprofessional players, and it is your job to prove that you are not one of those.

Once you have the reader's card in hand, go to the locker room and store your belongings. Bring into the reading room only the items that you need for your work and that are allowed there. Typically those items are your laptop or notebook, a pencil, your plastic ruler, your passport, your cell phone, and—if you depend on them—the books you need to understand the language and the layout of the manuscript. It can be a good idea to scan the relevant sections of such books ahead of time, as some collections may not allow you to bring physical books into the reading room. At some collections you may be offered see-through plastic bags for your gear to facilitate easy inspection as you enter and exit the reading room. If the locker area is large, you might want to take a quick picture of the number of your locker so that you can easily find your stored belongings at the end of your visit.

If you have arrived at a smaller or less research-intensive collection, the best tip is to approach the front desk. Introduce yourself and let them know about your appointment. The staff will most commonly register your presence and make sure you are familiar with the rules that apply in the reading room before guiding you to the locker room. Bring your essential tools with you to the reading room in agreement with the guidelines of the institution.

If your destination is a heritage collection, the most likely scenario is that you will be met by the person you have been in touch with via email. On these occasions, the most important guideline is to let your host take the lead and to be humble. Take it slow, listen carefully to the instructions you are given, and use your social skills to make sure you do not transgress the norms of the guardians of the manuscripts. You are their guest. Act like one.

We have yet to arrive at a collection where the procedures are precisely the same as in other collections. Each collection has its peculiarities, and getting some of the procedures wrong is easy. You may make mistakes, be corrected, or be bossed around. Take a deep breath, accommodate, and move on.

Entering the Reading Room and Getting Established at Your Desk

Entering a reading room in a major collection may be exciting, awe-inducing, or even somewhat frightening. Some reading rooms hint at past splendor—often with colonial undertones. Some evoke old-school academic or monastic virtues. Others are examples of mid-twentieth-century brutalist or functionalist architecture. Some are intimate, almost crypt-like; others

In the Reading Room with Your Manuscript 111

may remind you of the reading rooms in the university library back home. How you experience the surroundings may depend, for example, on whether you feel that you belong in the space or aspire to belong to the world it evokes.

When you find your bearings, approach the staff, introduce yourself, and tell them what you are there to see. They will show you where to sit. Sometimes, if you have requested to see a rare or particularly valuable manuscript, they may place you right in front of their desk or in a special rare-book section with added security. The most likely scenario, though, is that you will be asked to take a seat among the other readers.

If you have pre-ordered the manuscript you would like to see—either via email communication with the curators or by filling out digital forms—the manuscript has already been brought from the archives and is waiting for you. If not, you will be asked to order your manuscript now. Depending on the collection, ordering is done digitally or by filling in paper slips. To fill in these forms, you need to know both the shelfmark of the manuscript you want and your desk number. Be prepared to wait. It may take a while for the manuscript to arrive. The staff have many readers to care for, and there may be set hours for ordering manuscripts from the archives. In some collections, the staff will bring the manuscript to your desk. In others, you are expected to collect the manuscript from the staff and carry it to your desk yourself. When in doubt, ask politely or observe those around you and see what they are doing.

If you are visiting a smaller collection, the library where the manuscripts are kept may also serve as the reading room. Alternatively, your host may guide you to an office. Follow your host, and listen to any instructions. Since you were in touch with your host before you arrived, the manuscript is probably waiting for you.

Once you are settled at your desk, bring out your laptop or your notebook and the rest of your gear. Often you can also

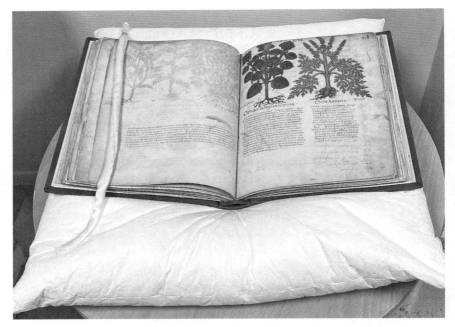

Figure 5.1. A facsimile codex positioned on a cushion for support with a snake weight helping to hold the codex open. (Photo by Brent Nongbri.)

bring a copy of the collection catalog to your desk or access it digitally. Your desk may already have a lectern, cradle, or cushion (beanbag or foam) to rest the manuscript on. If you have come to work on a codex, you will need one of those. The use of cushions or foam wedges reduces the stress on the sewing structures and protects the spine of the codex from breaking when you open it (Figure 5.1).

Most collections also provide **snake weights** (sometimes just called "snakes")—beaded cords covered in fabric—for keeping the leaves of the codex open at your chosen pages (see Figure 5.1). Other collections may have wooden sticks for this purpose. Such aids make reading easier and keep

In the Reading Room with Your Manuscript

you from handling the leaves unnecessarily. If none of this equipment is at your desk, ask the staff or your host whether it is available.

If you are working on papyri or other fragmentary material, chances are your manuscript will be mounted between panes of glass. Different institutions have different rules about handling these. In some collections, you are free to pick up the framed material, turn it over, tilt it for a different lighting angle, and generally to move it around as you please. In other collections, you may be asked to call on a curator or another member of the library staff to make any adjustments to the frame. When in doubt, ask.

If you are free to move the framed manuscript, be aware that glass frames can become quite heavy, especially if you are dealing with extensive fragments from a long roll. Be aware of the limitations of your own strength and grip— especially if you are asked to wear gloves (Box 5.1). If you need assistance, ask for it. Use extra caution if the fragments do not seem to be mounted securely. It is not uncommon to encounter cracked glass or fragments that are clearly moving between the panes of glass, especially if you are working with fragments mounted a long time ago. If you see cracks or movement, you may still move and flip the frame carefully, but do let the staff know so that the manuscript can be flagged for conservation.

It goes without saying, but we say it anyway: Do not bring any food or beverages into the reading room. And, although photographs of the pioneers who explored the Nag Hammadi codices and Dead Sea Scrolls in the mid-twentieth century frequently capture them with a cigarette between their lips (Figure 5.2), you will certainly not follow their lead and smoke or vape in the reading room! Remember that you are responsible for the well-being of the manuscript while it rests on your desk.

BOX 5.1. Gloves

Some collections require you to wear cotton gloves when handling the manuscripts. Others request that you do not. Still others have not made up their minds. The argument for wearing gloves is that the natural oils, and potentially the dirt, on your hands could leave stains. Those who argue against wearing gloves recognize that you need all the sensitivity of your fingers and hands to treat the manuscript as safely as possible. Gloves reduce that sensitivity and increase the risk of damage to the artifact.

If you find yourself in a collection that requires you to wear gloves, the staff in the reading room will probably lend you a pair. If you are a small person, you will typically find that the pair they offer is too large. Please note that oversized gloves will increase the risk of damage to the manuscript, so do not hesitate to ask for a smaller pair. Chances are that the gloves are unisize. Ask anyway, since your request may inspire the institution to purchase smaller pairs. Alternatively, bring your own properly fitting pair of cotton gloves. They are available online at reasonable prices.

If you are visiting a collection that does not require you to wear gloves, make absolutely sure that your hands are clean before you start handling a manuscript. You should not wear hand cream or nail polish. Both may stain the manuscript.

Ways of Looking at a Manuscript

Finally, you are at your desk with the manuscript you have been longing to see. How do you proceed? The answer depends on what your interests and research questions are and what

FIGURE 5.2. Gerald Lankaster Harding at work on the Dead Sea Scrolls in 1953 while smoking a cigarette. (Ronald Startup / Stringer / Picture Post via Getty Images.)

artifact you have arrived at the collection to see. Since the study of material texts are at the heart of this guidebook, the procedures we describe below presuppose that you are in the reading room to perform a three-dimensional study of texts-in-manuscripts (Box 5.2). You are examining a *manuscript* and not (only) reading a *text*. At the same time, we do not assume that you are a trained codicologist.

Whatever you do, we encourage you to use all your senses and celebrate the fact that you have not only visual but also perhaps tactile and even olfactory access to a material artifact of considerable age. In general, go in with specific goals, but be open to unexpected discoveries. Manuscript study almost always comes with some nice surprises.

> ### BOX 5.2. Aspects of Manuscripts to Observe
>
> - The materials of manuscripts: supports, format, size, binding elements, quires, etc.
> - Layout, organization, and structure: the number of columns, the number of lines per column, the size of margins, pricking and ruling, script, quire signatures, page numbers, delimitation markers, decorative elements, etc.
> - Contents: the inclusion and organization of individual works, subsections and collections, titles and other paratextual information, colophons, etc.
> - Signs of use and handling: corrections, additional notes, doodles, fingerprints, wax, damage patterns (mold, water, tears, pests, fire), traces of repair (patches of papyrus or parchment, stitched holes, replacement folia), etc.

Four Hypothetical Cases

In the following, we present four hypothetical cases. Each of these cases requires different procedures and different levels of engagement with the manuscript. Your particular research interest should determine how you proceed, and you may of course use strategies from more than one case.

CASE 1: IDENTIFYING AND CONTEXTUALIZING A TEXTUAL VARIANT IN A CODEX

Let us say that the apparatus of the critical edition you have been working on mentions a variant reading—a single but salient word—in one of the manuscripts that serve as witnesses to the text you study. The manuscript, a parchment codex, is

In the Reading Room with Your Manuscript 117

not digitized, and the images you have been able to dig up are either blurry or do not cover the specific pages that interest you. Unfortunately, obscure or missing images are still very common. You are eager to verify that the variant reading is in fact there. Also, you wonder if the manuscript may reveal more information about the variant.

In Liv's experience, it is always smart to start by making general observations about the artifact itself before turning to the pages of interest. By "general observations" we mean any relevant areas mentioned in Box 5.2—materials, layout, contents, signs of use—in addition to any available notes on the dating and provenance of the manuscript. However, Liv knows from her own encounters with manuscripts that you will probably move directly to the page where the variant is supposed to occur and figure it out at once. Go ahead! You can return to the systematic study of the artifact afterward.

Once you have located the page, what do you see? Give yourself a moment to decipher a script that might not be entirely familiar to you (Box 5.3).

Let's say that your autoptic inspection verifies that the variant reading is indeed there. On some occasions, that is all the information you will be able to take away from your inspection of the manuscript. The text in the column is there in neat orderliness, including the variant simply as part of the text that was copied.

However, on other occasions, your inspection may reveal something more interesting. Maybe you discover that the variant reading in your parchment codex is written on top of an erasure. The copyist or someone else has used a sharp tool to erase a word that was formerly there in order to correct the text. Such erasures leave scars in the top layer of the parchment and are relatively easy to spot. They indicate that the copyist or a later corrector made a conscious decision to replace the

BOX 5.3. Paleography

Paleography is, broadly speaking, the analysis of handwriting. The ability to recognize and analyze scripts is learned over time with exposure to many manuscripts. It cannot be mastered overnight, but with some practice, you can gain some sense of the different families of scripts in various languages.

There are general questions that you should ask about any script you encounter: Are the letters produced in a regular fashion, or is the same letter written in different ways? Does the writing strike you as neat or messy? Formal or informal? Do the letters appear to be written quickly and competently or slowly and with great labor? Can the letter forms and overall appearance of the script be classified as an example of a style that scholars recognize? Your answers to these kinds of questions can provide clues to the intentions of the copyist.

More detailed knowledge can be gained through the many paleographic handbooks that exist for different scripts. There is also a growing set of online resources for the study of ancient scripts, and these are in many ways superior to the old handbooks. The images in printed paleographic handbooks are sometimes not of the highest quality, and all but the most recent books can contain outdated information. Online resources, on the other hand, are often more current and better illustrated. For instance, the Vatican Library has excellent, up-to-date introductory websites that treat Greek and Latin paleography (https://spotlight.vatlib.it/greek-paleography and https://spotlight.vatlib.it/latin-paleography). It will probably not surprise you to learn that these sites have excellent illustrations. The same is true of the sites for Arabic, Latin, and

Syriac paleography at the HMML School website (https://hmmlschool.org/). The DASH portal at Stanford University provides access to digital images of Syriac manuscripts and computer assisted paleography (https://dash.stanford.edu/).

You can also find active ways to practice paleographic skills on the Internet—for example, at MultiPal (https://www.multipal.fr/en/welcome/), an interactive online tutorial on the first stages of reading several different scripts: Latin, Greek, Coptic, Hebrew, Aramaic, Syriac, and Sanskrit, among others.

word. Maybe you find dots, short lines, or other signs over, under, or encircling the word. Check also for any symbols close to the line in the margin. Any such markings suggest that an active reader has been aware that this is a variant and marked it to alert later readers. Or maybe you find out that someone has inscribed a note next to the line that includes the variant. What does it say? Are you looking at a correction or a comment by a later reader? Is it a text-critical note indicating that the reader acknowledged the variance in the text tradition (Figure 5.3; Box 5.4)?

This may be the point when you realize that you need to turn to the rest of the codex to situate and understand the variant in the context of the larger codex. Leaf gently through it and check if the treatment of your variant is part of a larger system of corrections or marginal comments that active readers have offered later readers. If so, you are looking at the textual practices of people that came before you, and you may appreciate that you are part of a longstanding critical engagement with the texts.

If you are lucky, the manuscript has a colophon or additional notes inscribed by copyists, donors, binders, correc-

FIGURE 5.3. A page from Codex Vaticanus showing a scribal note accompanying a correction to Hebrews 1:3: Vatican City, Biblioteca Apostolica Vaticana, Gr. 1209, page 1512. (Image reproduced by permission of Biblioteca Apostolica Vaticana, with all rights reserved. © 2024 Biblioteca Apostolica Vaticana.)

In the Reading Room with Your Manuscript

BOX 5.4. A Scribal Note about a Textual Variant

An especially vivid example of scribal interaction with a textual variant can be found in Codex Vaticanus (Vatican City, Biblioteca Apostolica Vaticana, Gr. 1209, page 1512), a pandect copy of the Bible in Greek generally assigned to the fourth century CE.

The manuscript as it now stands seems to preserve evidence of multiple changes to the text of Hebrews 1:3 (see Figure 5.3). The original copyist of Hebrews 1:3 wrote φανερῶν (*phanerōn*): Christ *"makes manifest* all things through his powerful word." A later user erased that word and replaced it with φέρων (*pherōn*), the reading more commonly found in this passage: Christ *"sustains* all things through his powerful word." Finally, an even later user of the codex erased the "corrected" version, restored the original φανερῶν, and added a note in the margin addressed to the first "corrector": ἀμαθέστατε καὶ κακέ, ἄφες τὸν παλαιόν, μὴ μεταποίει ("Fool and evil person, leave the old [reading] alone and don't change [it]!").

---

tors, owners, or others. These notes can sometimes provide information about reader interaction with the manuscript. If you are very lucky, one or more of these later users may even identify themselves and/or explicitly state the purpose of their engagement. That is the case in, for example, London, British Library, Add. Ms. 14,687, a lectionary manuscript in which an active reader states that he has added dotting (*rukokho* and *qushoyo*) to the Syriac script to ensure that later readers pronounce the so-called *begadkephat*-consonants correctly.

Now, go back to the critical edition you have used so far and assess how it has made information available to you and, potentially, what information it has left out. You may also realize that studying variants is not only a relevant part of a diachronic study of textual history, which is primarily what the apparatus in a critical edition offers you, but also part of an invested study of patterns in particular manuscripts and of reader engagement with specific cultural artifacts.

CASE 2: INVESTIGATING A PARTICULAR COPY OF A TEXT IN A CODEX

Let us imagine that when you arrive at the reading room, your only information is that the text you are working on is part of a specific codex. You know the shelfmark and the language / manuscript tradition it belongs to, and you also know that the codex is medieval, but you don't know what other texts it contains or whether your text is part of a traditional corpus. This may be the situation if your manuscript is not yet properly cataloged or if the existing catalog contains a bare minimum of information. You aim to find out what the codex and its collection of books may tell you about the identification and function of the text in this particular manuscript.

If this is your aim, many features of the codex are potentially relevant. Depending on the manuscript you have in front of you, you may find either that your goal is relatively easy to achieve or that you are in for some detective work. The following procedure can be helpful if you decide to explore the codex systematically.

Start by having a good look at the artifact in front of you. Consider the size of the bound codex. Is it, for example, a large tome—a deluxe codex—or a smaller, utilitarian-sized artifact? Sometimes the size may give you a first indication about the status of the codex or the use it was intended for. For exam-

In the Reading Room with Your Manuscript

ple, the functions of a deluxe codex were different from those of a miniature codex. However, if the size of the codex falls within the standard, utilitarian range, the measurements alone may not offer you a lead.

Move on to inspecting the binding. If the manuscript in front of you has a medieval binding, it may provide information about, for example, the value former owners ascribed to the codex and sometimes also the environment to which the manuscript belonged. However, in all likelihood, the binding you are looking at is modern. Bindings wear out and must be replaced regularly, and the manuscripts that arrived in Europe from the Middle East and Africa in the eighteenth and nineteenth centuries were routinely rebound at arrival. This means that the binding is probably not going to provide you with information that will help you reach your goal.

Open the binding, make sure that the codex rests comfortably on the lectern, cradle, or cushion, and use snake weights or wooden sticks to keep it open. Bring out your ruler again and measure the size of the book block. Measuring is usually associated with science, but it is also an art. When you take a measurement, be sure to record in your notes the exact point at which you took it. If possible, take a photograph with the scale included. If you later need to compare your measurements with the measurements of others, it will be useful to have as much **metadata** as possible about your own measurements in case you need to explain any discrepancies.

If you are lucky, the outer folia of the book block are intact. Depending on the type of codex you are working on and the manuscript tradition to which it belongs, these pages may carry important information. Sometimes a **superscript title** or a title page will tell you how those who produced the codex identified its contents. Yet other times a colophon at the end of the inscribed text on one of the final pages (and sometimes at the end of a subsection within the codex) may provide information about the corpus.

Unfortunately, the outermost folia of a book block are particularly vulnerable to wear and tear. They are often damaged, missing, or have been replaced at a later time. If this is the case for the manuscript you are exploring, essential information about the codex is lost. Your hunt for the identity of the collection in the codex and the role of the specific text within it has to depend on information in other parts of the book block. In that case, leaf carefully through the codex and identify how the copyist or someone else in the production team marked the ends and the beginnings of the individual books. On some occasions, titles identify beginning and/or end. On other occasions, copyists distinguished the first letter or the first words of a new layout unit by color or size (creating an **incipit**). Sometimes they skipped lines, leaving a space between books, or added decorative features to help readers navigate. Some manuscripts contain, for example, an illumination to mark the beginning of a new book, while others are sparsely decorated. Identifying the way the codex systematizes its literary units may help you answer the question as to what collection of texts the codex contains.

Note, though, that many codices will make your investigation of the collection structure both more difficult and more interesting. Some codices have a miscellaneous character: they do not contain a collection of texts that is identifiable as a traditional collection, such as "Gospels" or "Prophets," or works ascribed to a certain authorial figure. Rather, these miscellaneous codices may reflect the wishes of the persons who procured the codex or the needs of a certain monastery. Even more interesting are **composite codices**, books made up of discrete codicological units of different origins. Sometimes the consti-

In the Reading Room with Your Manuscript

tution of a bound unit changed over time. Sometimes book blocks that once made up discrete units were later bound together, or quires originating with other codices were repurposed and bound together to form a new book block. The result is a codex that has grown and that displays a form of archaeological layering. At other times, a singular bound unit was at some point split in two. When you aim to study the codex context of a given text, you need to remember that this context may have been dynamic and that the context as it now sits in front of you represents just one moment in a diachronic development.

Finally, turn to the copy of the text you came to explore. Find out where in the codex it is located and what other books the copyist copied in its immediate proximity. Sometimes the location of the copy in the codex provides a clue. For example, a text copied at the very end of a codex was sometimes inscribed there because a folio offered just the right amount of available writing surface or offered a space simply to preserve the text from oblivion. In these cases, the identity of the collection copied in the codex may not shed much light on the perceived identity of the particular text. Texts copied at the end were sometimes also understood as marginally part of, or as additions to, the collection in the codex. Pay particular attention to the script and page layout of texts located in such positions. Does the text that interests you share the same layout and script as the other texts or is it singled out in any way?

Move on to the titles. How do initial or end titles identify the book you are interested in, and do the titles of adjacent books suggest kinship between these texts? The study of such additional written features on the page (paratexts) may turn out to be your most important sources. They provide you with information about the identification of discrete copies of texts and sometimes about the collection formation in the codex.

If you assume that codices are generally not haphazard collections but that they served as purposeful artifacts to their producers, procurers, and users, answering these questions may help you reach your goal of establishing the identification and function of your text in this particular codex context. How do your newly acquired insights about the manuscript context of the text affect your interpretation of it?

CASE 3: STUDYING A FRAGMENT OF UNCERTAIN FORMAT

Cases 1 and 2 above provide you with some approaches to examining a relatively complete codex. In those situations, you are confronted with almost an overload of data to try to digest in an organized way. When dealing with more fragmentary remains, the exercise at times becomes one of disciplined imagination. If you are looking at the fragmentary remains of a codex folium now mounted between glass panes, you must use what you observe to try to imagine what the three-dimensional codex was like. Do you see any elements of the binding? Are there any traces of page numbers that could provide a clue to how thick the codex was? If you are looking at the fragmentary remains of a roll, the same type of imagination is required. What did the roll from which these fragments came look like when it was produced? Are margins preserved that could allow you to reconstruct the height of the roll?

Sometimes, however, fragmentary remains can present questions that are even more fundamental. It may not be clear whether you are dealing with the remains of a codex, the remains of a roll, or the remains of a single sheet. Let's say that one of the texts that interests you is preserved on a substantial papyrus fragment—about 20 centimeters high and 12 centimeters wide (about 8⅞ by 4¾ inches). The text is copied on

In the Reading Room with Your Manuscript 127

the "front" of the papyrus, along the fibers. There is also writing on the back of the papyrus, copied against the grain of the vertical fibers. It is more abraded and difficult to read. It can't be identified with certainty as part of your text, but a few words are legible here and there. You may wish to know if this papyrus represents a continuous, complete copy of your text or if it is instead an excerpt or a smaller portion of your text. How might you be able to tell whether you are dealing with a copy of your text on a roll, a copy on a codex folium, or a short selection on a loose sheet of papyrus, perhaps an amulet or memory aid?

What kind of clues can you look for to determine format? There are some fairly easy tests that are good places to start. Any traces of a page number at the top or bottom of the fragment would be an indicator that you have the remains of a folium from a codex. What is the orientation of the writing on the back of the papyrus? Is it right side up or upside down relative to the writing on the front? If it is upside down, you are most likely dealing with a roll or a sheet and not a folium from a codex. Is the writing on the back of the papyrus in the same script as the writing on the front? If so, there is a good chance that this is a codex, although opisthograph roll, though less common, would also be a possibility. If the script used to copy the text on the back of the papyrus is definitely different from the script on the front, the papyrus may be a reused roll or sheet, but you may instead have before you a folium from a codex that was copied by more than one copyist. This is especially a possibility if the text on the front of the papyrus happens to be at or near the end of a work. It may be that a new work was inscribed by a different copyist on the verso of a codex folium.

Other clues can be helpful but more ambiguous. How is the text laid out on the page? Is there more than one column?

128   In the Reading Room with Your Manuscript

If so, the text may occur in a roll, although papyrus codices with multiple columns of text to the page do exist. More telling would be any traces of the spacing between the columns. Codex pages often have larger outer margins than inner margins, and in codices with multiple columns of text per page, the space between columns (the intercolumn) is usually smaller than either the inner or the outer margin. Such uneven spacing would be evidence in favor of a codex. And of course, indications of the same kind of writing in columns and spacing on the back of the papyrus would be further evidence that you are working on a codex folium. If there are any remains of any *kollēseis,* then you can know that your fragment was part of a roll at one point in time, but remember that the papyrus used for codex bifolia was usually cut from blank rolls, so this kind of evidence is not decisive for format.

As you can see, you may get lucky and find clear evidence that helps you make a firm judgment on the format of the fragmentary papyrus that carries your text. Or you might very well not be able to determine the format with certainty. Ambiguity is perfectly normal. Working on fragmentary material almost always involves cumulative evidence and probabilities.

CASE 4: WORKING ON A FRAGMENTARY MANUSCRIPT

Sometimes your critical edition itself will practically beg you to have a close look at a manuscript. Such invitations in the Nestle-Aland edition of the Greek New Testament take the form of the superscript letters "vid" after a witness abbreviation in the manuscript.[1] As the introduction of the Nestle-Aland indicates, "vid" stands for the Latin phrase *ut videtur* ("as it appears"), meaning that the reading reported for the manuscript is probable but not certain. This designation occurs

In the Reading Room with Your Manuscript 129

well over a thousand times in the apparatus of the twenty-eighth edition of the Nestle-Aland. If a given reading is important for your research and is marked in a manuscript as probable but not certain, you may well ask yourself just how probable that reading actually is.

Often you can answer such questions by working with a digital image, but on other occasions, you might find that consulting the manuscript in person is necessary. Consider the case of a simple textual variant in Matthew 19:10. Some manuscripts read οἱ μαθηταί ("the disciples"), some read οἱ μαθηταὶ αὐτοῦ ("his disciples"), and the Nestle-Aland prints οἱ μαθηταὶ [αὐτοῦ] ("[his] disciples"). One of the manuscripts listed in support of the absence of αὐτοῦ is 𝔓[71vid]. This is P.Oxy. XXIV 2385, kept at the Bodleian Art, Archaeology, and Ancient World Library in Oxford. The relevant side of the papyrus is the front (the portion written along the horizontal fibers). The published edition of this fragment reads as follows (brackets indicate letters supplied by the editor; dots beneath letters indicate that the letters are only partially visible):

$$[\lambda\epsilon\text{-}]$$
$$[\gamma o]\underset{.}{\upsilon}[\sigma\iota\nu]\ \alpha\underset{.}{\upsilon}[\underset{.}{\tau}\omega]\ \underset{.}{o}\underset{.}{\iota}\ \mu\underset{.}{\alpha}[\theta\eta\tau\alpha\iota$$
$$\epsilon\iota\ o\upsilon\tau\omega\varsigma\ \epsilon\sigma\tau\iota\nu\ \alpha\iota\tau\iota\alpha\ \tau o[\upsilon\ \alpha\nu o\upsilon$$
$$[\mu\epsilon\tau\alpha\ \tau]\eta\varsigma\ \gamma\upsilon\nu\alpha\iota\kappa o\varsigma\ [o\upsilon\ \sigma\upsilon\mu\text{-}$$
$$[\varphi\epsilon]\rho[\epsilon\iota]\ \gamma\alpha\mu\eta\sigma\alpha\iota\ o\ \delta\epsilon\ [\epsilon\iota\pi\epsilon\nu$$
$$[\alpha\upsilon]\tau o\iota\varsigma\ o\upsilon\ \pi\alpha\nu\tau\epsilon\varsigma\ \chi\omega[\rho o\upsilon\sigma\iota\nu$$

The brackets and sublinear dots in the transcription show that the relevant portion of the text is poorly preserved. If we look at an image of the manuscript, the problem becomes a bit more vivid (Figure 5.4).

Only very small traces of the letters in the words οἱ μαθηταί survive at the top of the fragment, and the editor of

Figure 5.4. A papyrus fragment showing faint traces of writing along the top edge: P.Oxy. XXIV 2385. (Image courtesy of The Egypt Exploration Society. © The Egypt Exploration Society; the content is protected by UK law.)

the papyrus notes that reconstructing the line arrangement has been difficult. The number of letters per line reconstructed on this side of the papyrus is not the same as the number of letters per line reconstructed on the other side of the papyrus. To make the proposed arrangement work, the editor had to reconstruct one line as an instance of ekthesis, although there is no relevant sense break in this portion of the text. Could the ink traces at the top of the fragment be interpreted differently? Could alternative reconstructions of the text be possible? Perhaps even one in which the allegedly missing word is present?

Digital images can be helpful in experimenting with possible reconstructions. Zooming in on high-resolution images can allow you to see the questionable areas with great clarity. Photo-editing software allows you to copy and paste the copyist's own letters to attempt to fill in **lacunae** in different ways.

In the Reading Room with Your Manuscript

Do you need to examine such a fragment in person? There may be good reasons to do so. Putting a fragment under a microscope can be very helpful with these kinds of problems, sometimes even more helpful than zooming in on a good digital image. If you have access to something like a Dino-Lite microscope with different modes of illumination, infrared light can be especially useful in detecting obscured traces of carbon-based inks.

It is also possible that folded fibers in the papyrus conceal traces of writing. Especially in the early days of papyrology, many editors aimed to work quickly and efficiently to publish the texts in their manuscripts and may not have had the assistance of expert conservators. As a result, papyri in some collections are framed with creases or with loose fibers folded over in positions that obscure traces of letters. If you are able to identify such a case of misplaced fibers during your examination, you can alert the staff in the reading room, who may be able to connect you with a conservator to open the frame and adjust the fibers for you. This may not be possible to accomplish on short notice, but in any event, be sure to record such details in your own notes for future reference or future visits.

Taking Notes and Pictures

An important aspect of your work is to ensure that you record all the information you need for your research in a way that makes it retrievable once you are back home. You may choose to take notes on your laptop or in a notebook (using a pencil, not a pen). A rule of thumb is to record any relevant information about the manuscript that is not covered by the catalog entry. Always err on the side of taking too many notes. The regret will be great if you later find that your notes are too sparse. Also, always note features of the manuscript that you do not understand. Make sure that your notes also reflect the difference between information that you are certain about and reflections that are hypothetical only.

Not all collections allow picture taking, but if they do, take pictures. Images are tremendously helpful when you return home. The key to a helpful set of images is to acknowledge the frailty of your memory. Do not assume that you will remember what page or even what manuscript a picture stems from. In Chapter 6 we show you how to organize your images and how to add metadata to digital images when your stay at the collection is over. However, the task of providing a good set of images starts when you are sitting at the desk with the manuscript.

A good idea is to take pictures in a predefined order. Start with a picture of the exterior of the artifact and the shelfmark or call number. This picture helps you identify which manuscript the images that follow belong to. Next, even if you are interested in a small detail in the lower left section of the outer column, start with an image of the entire page before you take the close-up. This image will provide you with both information about the folio number (if it is recorded on the page) and the context the detail appears in on that page. Then repeat the procedure when you turn to the next detail. This procedure provides you with an orderly set of images that is easy to transport to other devices and that does not allow for any confusion. You are also making sure to systematically preserve the all-important contextual information.

When You Need a Break

Did you know that many professional chess players work out on an athletic level? This may sound surprising at first, given that they just sit to play chess, but sitting for long hours bent

In the Reading Room with Your Manuscript

over the chessboard in intense concentration is in fact physically demanding. So is manuscript study! When your body tells you to take a break—do it. As lunch is closing in or at the end of the day, your concentration level drops. At this point, you need to be extra careful. The worst thing you can do is to rush. If you rush, you will not do your work properly, and you may even end up putting the manuscript at risk. Perhaps it is time for a meal? And do remember to keep yourself nicely caffeinated.

What do you do when you leave your desk? Again, the rules vary, but leaving the manuscript unattended is not acceptable at most collections. Bring it back to the front desk and tell the staff that you are not finished with it, only taking a break. When you leave the reading room, a guard may routinely look through your bag to make sure that you do not bring anything besides your own belongings out of the room.

Accessing Archival Records in the Reading Room

In Chapter 3 we addressed the importance of exploring the acquisition and ownership history of the manuscripts you are interested in, so you are probably already quite familiar with the provenance details of your manuscript. However, as part of your on-site research, you may also have the opportunity to access the archival records of the owning institution. They can be a rich source of knowledge about the life of the manuscript you are studying. Ask the staff whether they are aware of more information about the history of the manuscripts beyond what is available in the online catalog. Some collections keep quite detailed records about who has examined a manuscript. You can sometimes learn which scholars and conservators have worked with the manuscript before you encountered it. It may also be a good idea to go carefully through the bookshelves in the reading room. You may come across old catalogs that you were not familiar with or other books that contain the information you are looking for. Scanning shelves can be a good use of your time if you find yourself having to wait for long periods for the delivery of your manuscripts.

Sometimes, the pastedowns and **flyleaves** of a codex include notes from modern owners, curators, and scholars. On one occasion, Liv came across a letter from the person who brought the manuscript to Europe: it was bound with the codex (London, British Library, Or. 8732). If the codex came to your desk in a protective cardboard box, check whether the box contains flyers or information sheets carrying additional information. If you are working on papyri or other material mounted in glass frames, be aware of the labeling on the frames. You can sometimes find interesting information that is usually cropped out of published photographic plates. You may also come to be familiar with certain styles of mounting and conservation, which can allow you to tentatively identify items that may have been mounted by the same conservator.

Reading Rooms Are Social Spaces

If you have never been to a reading room before, you may not imagine them as social spaces. True, you spend most of your time in the reading room working alone, focused exclusively on the manuscript in front of you, but you will also interact with curators and library staff, manuscript guardians, and other readers.

Your interactions with staff will vary, depending on the collection you are visiting. In some large collections, the staff serve many readers and will not be able to assist you more than others. In other, smaller and less research-intensive collections, an academic librarian, curator, or guardian may have spent both time and effort preparing for your stay. The staff person may even spend the day in the reading room because you are there. On some occasions, you may even be set up to work in a curator's personal office. Make sure to acknowledge such generosity.

Sometimes you may also be in touch with other readers. You may spot that another reader is working on materials similar to your own, or you may strike up a conversation in the coffee line. Other readers may also be in touch with you. In the reading room, you may have the opportunity to establish relationships with curators and readers that will benefit you (and hopefully them) for years to come. At the same time, notions of social hierarchies and conceptions about the ideal academic professional are at play. Be aware that in some settings, gender roles and cultural stereotypes can affect your interactions both with library staff and with other readers.

Although you will be diligently working on your materials during a research visit, remember to pause every once in a while to savor the moment. For many of us, working on these items is the culmination of years of preparation.

Further Reading

Adcock, Edward P., ed. *IFLA Principles for the Care and Handling of Library Material*. Paris: IFLA, 2019. Open access: https://www.ifla.org/wp-content/uploads/2019/05/assets/pac/ipi/ipi1-en.pdf.

Cuellar, Gregory L. *Empire, the British Museum, and the Making of the Biblical Scholar in the Nineteenth Century*. London: Palgrave Macmillan, 2019.

Farge, Arlette. *The Allure of the Archives*. New Haven: Yale University Press, 2015.

6

Back Home—What Now?

When you are back home after a research trip to a museum or an archive, it is very easy to lose the momentum built up from the excitement of the visit. The daily routine of life sets in. The massive amount of collected data can seem daunting, and there the data sits. This chapter offers some practical tips to make the most of the material you collected during your manuscript research trip and to minimize lost time and data.

This process doesn't necessarily need to wait until you are back home. If you used public transportation of some kind to get to your collection, buses, trains, and planes can sometimes be good places to get focused work done. If you resist the temptation to use available wireless connections and have no distractions from other passengers, getting out your laptop and working on your documentation can be a good way to spend the trip.

Organize Your Images

It is best to organize your data as soon as possible after you collect it. If you are able to make your own digital images, it can even be a good idea to carry out some of this organization

Back Home—What Now?

in the evenings during your research trip. But maintaining balance is also important: while you are away, you don't want to burn yourself out. Finding yourself without sufficient time, energy, or motivation to do a thorough job of organizing your materials while you are on site is perfectly normal. But the task of organization should be undertaken as soon as possible upon your arrival back home. Organizing your material is, of course, a challenge, because now all the responsibilities of normal life come flooding back—chores, work, family, bills, and so forth.

So what can you do to keep things organized? You may have returned with hundreds of similar-looking pictures. Your camera probably provides your first line of organization in the form of file names that are sequentially numbered. But you will want to add more detail to your images by means of metadata to make the images easily findable with standard search features on laptops and other devices. Adding metadata to digital images used to be a long and somewhat tiresome process, but newer devices offer smoother and more intuitive ways to do it. And that is a good thing, because data management is important. You definitely want to avoid seeing, a few months after your visit, a series of images that you know were important but cannot recall the reason why.

The first question, then, is "What kind of metadata should I add to images?" and the second question is "How do I add metadata to the images?"

Most digital cameras automatically add the date and time an image was made. Phone cameras often add the location as well if geolocation services are activated. What you need to add are the details that will help make the photos useful to you. Adding tags and keywords to make the photos easily searchable is a good way to proceed. You might begin by adding the institution (library or museum) and shelfmark of the manuscript. If you have taken images of multiple pages from a single codex or multiple columns from a single roll, you may want to add the page number or column number. If the image includes a notable feature that you might want to be able to search across several different manuscripts—a peculiar abbreviation or decorative element, for example—that can be good to add as a keyword or a tag. You may also want to add notes about any special conditions that were in place. Was this photo taken with ambient lighting, or did you use raking light?

How to add metadata will depend on the devices you use and the way you interface with your images. If you took your pictures using a mobile phone, there are usually very simple methods to keep your pictures organized. We cannot give specialized instructions for every model of phone, but by searching online for the model of your phone and some variation of the phrase "add metadata to photos," you will very likely find detailed instructions for adding titles, captions, and keywords to your photos; for some models, you may find that the metadata must be entered through a laptop. If you took dozens of pictures of the same manuscript, reentering the shelfmark of the manuscript for every single image would be tedious. Be aware that most phones and tablets allow you to add metadata in batches. Again, searching online for your phone model and a phrase like "adding metadata to groups of photos" should turn up the relevant instructions for assigning captions and keywords to an entire group of images.

Sometimes you will want to add more specific information to certain images. The more specificity you add, the easier it will be to find what you need at a later point in time. Again, noting particular features that you tried to capture in the image can be helpful. If you took notes about these features in a word-processing document, adding the name of that document to the keywords may be a good idea. What you want to avoid is coming back to your images a few weeks (or months or years) later and wondering, "Why on earth did I take this picture?"

Back Home—What Now? 139

If you were not able to take your own photos but had to order them from the library or museum, you can follow these same steps to add metadata. Brent generally keeps separate folders of such ordered images together with a copy of the order form itself, which can be useful if at a later time there is a need to seek permission for use of one or more of the images (for more on this topic, see Chapter 8).

Organize Your Notes

In Chapter 5, we described some helpful ways of taking notes. It can also be useful to revisit your notes very soon after your visit. Make sure that you have given your notes file a good descriptive title. Brent always includes the name of the institution he visits and the date of his visit in the file name so that he can quickly and easily find the right document, even when he has made several visits to the same collection. So, for example, he has documents called:

Chester Beatty Library 2013 August.docx
Chester Beatty Library 2021 October.docx
Chester Beatty Library 2022 October.docx

On each of these visits, he viewed different materials, and it is helpful to keep track of what manuscripts were examined on which occasions. After his visits, he creates a kind of table of contents at the top of the document to give himself a quick overview of what the document contains. For example, on his first visit to what was then known as the Chester Beatty Library in Dublin, he was not allowed to take any pictures, so he ended up taking forty-five pages of detailed notes in a Word document. At the end of his trip, he wrote this quick summary of the contents of the document:

Chester Beatty Library
Materials examined:

- 12 August: Ac 1389 (P.Bodmer XXI); Ac 1499 (Greek grammar, Greco-Latin lexicon)
- 13 August: Ac 2556 (Letters of Pachomius); Ac 2554 (Panopolis tax codex)
- 14 August: Ac 2556 (Panopolis tax codex); K72 Memorandum; Kenyon papers
- 15 August: P46 10 folios plus 3 bifolia; Archival materials
- 16 August: P46 the rest of the folia not on display; Archival materials
- 19 August: P46 center of quire; Archival materials
- 20 August: P45 all leaves not on display
- 21 August: BP VII, Isaiah all intact bifolia and select others; Archival materials
- 22 August: Remaining BP, van Regemorter material
- 23 August: Remaining archival materials (Robinson, Edwards, Bell)

This practice makes it easy to see when you open the file whether the information you are seeking is likely to be in the document.

If at some point after a visit he wants to make changes to the notes he made, he never deletes anything permanently. Instead, he uses the ~~strike through~~ feature so that he has a visible record of his impressions at the time he was examining the materials. He also notes the date of any additional notes or observations that he adds to the file after the visit. Sometimes, too, he adds cross-references to any image files that are related to specific notes.

Finally, it is important to back up your data. Using a cloud service or an external hard drive, or preferably both, is always a good idea.

Fading Memory and Remediation

Immediately after a visit, you can feel a great deal of familiarity with the manuscripts you have studied. But that feeling inevitably fades with time. Human memory is a fragile thing. Your engagement with the manuscripts is now going to be mediated through your images, your notes, and maybe online digital images and published photographic facsimiles. Over time, you may discover discrepancies between these various remediations of your manuscripts. Sometimes these can be resolved. For instance, let's say you encounter something in a digital image you made that is different from something you see in a published photographic facsimile. It is always good to read all the front matter in facsimile editions, especially older ones. They can sometimes provide insight into the production of the facsimiles and perhaps suggest a solution to the incongruency. Here is a note found at the beginning of an early twentieth-century facsimile of a fragmentary papyrus codex: "The pages of the facsimile are entirely free from retouching and, in painting out *lacunae* and margins, the utmost pains were taken not to obscure any letter."[1] So we are reassured that the pages have not been retouched, but at the same time we are told that the empty spaces and margins have been "painted out." If our discrepancy has to do with, say, the shape of an edge of a folio or traces of a damaged letter near a hole in the papyrus, we might have found an explanation. On the other hand, the software in the cameras in mobile phones, especially more recent models, can manipulate images in certain ways automatically. Some of these software features can be disabled, but others cannot; checking online is the easiest way to find out. This may be another reason for a discrepancy between remediations.

How can you fix these kinds of problems? On your own, you may not be able to resolve contradictions between your notes and your photographs or between your photographs and a published facsimile. If so, you have some options. One of the reasons we advised you to make efforts to be polite and friendly to all the staff you encounter, aside from practicing common courtesy, is that they can be helpful allies in your research even after your visit. Although they are busy, most library staff will be happy to check a detail for you to confirm or disconfirm a certain specific question. But before crafting your email to the curators, jump ahead to Chapter 7 to see our advice about asking for help.

Striking While the Iron Is Hot vs. Letting an Idea Simmer

If everything went well with your visit, you collected the data that you needed to answer, or at least make good progress on, your research questions. But you may also have noticed any number of other interesting smaller details about the manuscripts you studied, and some of these might even be worth publishing about separately from your original project. Then you have a decision to make. Do you stay focused on your original research, which still may require a considerable amount of digesting and processing time, or do you set that aside and try to publish your unexpected finds, which may be more swiftly written up and sent off?

There are benefits and drawbacks to both choices. On the one hand, you can put these smaller ideas aside and stay focused on your main project. This approach has the benefit of keeping you on task, but you may risk never going back to those smaller but still interesting and worthwhile observations. Alternatively, you might strike while the iron is hot and write up one or more of these more manageable details for publication. The risk there is that you perhaps move too quickly, so your work is not as careful as it should be. Brent has written a few articles using this latter method. After making some unexpected discoveries, he wrote them up and sent drafts to experts to ask for feedback. In one case, the input he received was so thorough that he ended up co-authoring a piece with one of the experts he contacted. (There can be upsides and downsides to that kind of arrangement, but we'll treat this in more detail in Chapter 7.)

Further Reading

Seymour, Virginia. "Metadata for Image Search and Discovery," *JSTOR Daily,* May 25, 2023. Open access: https://daily.jstor.org/metadata-for-image-search-and-discovery/.

7
Asking for Help

When working with manuscripts, there will be things that you do not and cannot know, even after consulting the best reference tools and bibliographies. What is to be done when you encounter one of these roadblocks?

For a variety of reasons, a good deal of knowledge in Manuscript Studies remains unpublished, residing in the minds of seasoned experts. Most often, these experts are happy to share their knowledge, but their time is limited, and as expertise increases, so also does the amount of time dedicated to answering questions from people with less experience. This chapter offers strategies for recognizing when you need help and when you do not, for building a network that can assist you, and for learning how to contact an expert when help is needed—while keeping in mind that in a few years, you may well be the expert whose help is constantly being sought.

The Networking Champion

Liv was trained in the History of Religions and specialized in the study of early Jewish literature. However, back in 2005, she started to take an interest in the manuscript transmission

Asking for Help 145

of this literature. The text she was interested in, 2 Baruch, survives first and foremost in Syriac manuscripts, so she suddenly found herself devoted to a field of knowledge that she knew little about. In the years that followed, she read whatever relevant sources she could find, attended conferences, followed dedicated groups on social media, and got acquainted with scholars who specialize in Syriac manuscript study. Starting up a research project that demanded the acquisition of a substantial amount of new knowledge made her feel both humble and vulnerable. She felt like a first-year student again, and her questions were numerous. On many occasions, she was able to answer them herself by reading yet another article or by autoptically studying the manuscripts in question. Sometimes a question got answered several years after she first started pondering it. On yet other occasions, she was unable to find answers. When she started her studies, the guidebooks and reference tools in Syriac manuscript study were still relatively few, and, in addition, she was studying a text that was marginal to the tradition and that had received limited attention in previous research. She realized that if she was going to find answers to some of her inquiries, she had to ask for help.

The old stereotype of the solitary manuscript scholar is of a man lost in concentration, hunched over the piles of books on his desk (this imaginary scholar has indeed usually been a man). But this caricature has never been accurate. Surviving documentation shows that manuscript scholars have always been in touch with each other, and that includes women scholars. Before international travel became common and long before the Internet, scholars already relied on colleagues in other towns and countries to check details in manuscripts in local collections. They communicated by means of handwritten letters, collaborating over time despite wide geographical distances, and sometimes even acknowledged each other's services

146   Asking for Help

when they finally published their works. In other words, academic networks are no novelty.

During the past couple of decades, networking possibilities have increased astronomically, and the networking champions abound. Today's young academics increasingly cooperate with others both in person and online. They interact with colleagues in large research projects, networks, or professional societies, subscribe to email lists, talk with colleagues on social media, and share their knowledge in the chat functions of online manuscript portals. They know what a professor's favorite pet looks like, thanks to Instagram, and meet old and new friends at conferences and workshops, on- and off-line.

One of the first things you should do when you are new to a field is to establish what the main professional meeting places are: Which conferences are the up-and-coming academics attending, and which professional societies are they members of? You should become a member too. Move on to the digital scene: Which email lists should you subscribe to, which blogs or other digital portals are helpful to your area of research, who should you follow on social media, and which Facebook groups do your colleagues frequent? Scholars who take an interest in manuscripts could, for example, find that subscribing to the Agade email list is helpful (although it will very quickly fill up your inbox). If you work on papyrus manuscripts, the PAPY email list is useful. Although papyrologists were among the first ancient historians to embrace the technology of the computer, they are among the last to hold on to the email listserv. For scholars of Syriac manuscripts, the Hugoye list is invaluable—it connects a vibrant and friendly community. Some blogs can be worth following too, such as Brent Nongbri's *Variant Readings* (Liv recommends it!) and James R. Davila's *PaleoJudaica*. Worth following in social media are, for example, HMML, the Duke Manuscript Migration Lab, and

Asking for Help

the Princeton Geniza Lab. Check out Alin Suciu's Coptic Literature and Manuscripts, the New Testament Textual Criticism group, the North American Society for the Study of Christian Apocryphal Literature group, or the Follow the Pots group—depending on your research interests.

You should join these networks and follow these accounts, not primarily because you need help but because your colleagues share news there, and some major debates are playing out there, too. During the past decades, the pace of academic debate has accelerated, largely due to digital networked media. If you do not follow along, you will miss out on major discussions.

The contacts you establish in these forums may also be the ones who can offer you assistance when you encounter a difficulty in your study of a manuscript. These arenas are the place to go for some of your inquiries. If you suspect that access to an image of a manuscript page may solve a riddle, or if you wonder whether someone else has written about the issues you are struggling with, online forums may be the place to go. In many online academic communities, someone will provide an answer to your inquiry within minutes. A colleague in Australia may share images of a manuscript page with you, and a peer in Argentina may send you a PDF of an article that brings the last piece to your puzzle. Yet others may enter into discussion with you about an issue you have pondered, or you may learn from the questions that others pose or from the answers your colleagues offer them.

Before you ask for help or advice, spend some time figuring out what kinds of questions your colleagues are typically posing in the forum. Each forum has its own profile. Allow yourself to be a lurker for a while; learn from others; internalize the established style and way of engaging with your peers. And if someone happens to pose a question that you can answer, show the same generosity that you hope that a colleague will show you when you are in need of help.

These avenues are perfect for some of your questions but maybe not for all of them. Digital forums are public or semi-public spaces and will expose you to a certain level of vulnerability. You may have taken our advice and been lurking in these online spaces for a while. Take into account that many others are too. You do not always know who listens in, so you should not pose a question that you are not comfortable sharing publicly. You may not want to expose all your insecurities, either. How much you are willing to share is a personal, cultural, and generational issue: you must be okay with it. You may also not want to share your very best research ideas. Your questions may be more interesting than you were aware of, and the status of unpublished ideas and informal expressions shared online is vague. Suddenly your best ideas may become publicly available and thus up for grabs.

Learn from Liv. She has made all the mistakes. She has posed questions that were not well informed, gotten the genre wrong, shared too much, and seen one of her ideas suddenly everywhere. She is still ashamed of some of the interactions and frowns upon past-Liv for her naïveté. Still, she also knows that parts of her earlier interactions turned out to be very productive: she received advice that is still benefiting her, and she became part of supportive academic communities. If she had not shared her ideas, she would have shielded herself from new knowledge, from collegiality, and from ongoing discussions in her field. Brent, alternatively, has mostly avoided social media. As a result, he has been late to know about many academic discussions. On the other hand, he has also bypassed the unpleasantness that can easily churn up on social media platforms, and he has had one less set of notifications fighting for his time and attention. The bottom line is to use social media to the extent that it works for you.

Asking for Help 149

Emailing an Expert

Being active on social media is a choice, and not all academics have chosen to be. Partly this is a generational issue. Most senior scholars have an email account and a certain digital presence, but many of them elect not to participate in the larger repertoire of social media platforms. Keeping a low online profile may also be a matter of choice, and not only for senior scholars. Keeping track of social media takes time, and it may disrupt a work-life balance. In addition, many platforms have ownership structures, use algorithms, or allow forms of speech and interaction that are indeed problematic. Hence, many experts will not be available in online forums. In addition, some of them do not travel long distances, so you will not meet them in person at conferences either. Sometimes, then, if you need advice or information, your best option is to send an email.

Indeed, a good deal of knowledge about manuscripts never sees the light of day in a publication. Some manuscripts have been accessible only to a select group of scholars—for good or not so good reasons. Others are in languages that only a few experts master. Some manuscript traditions lack sufficient reference tools or even introductory textbooks. It also takes time to develop the skills and experience necessary to know a manuscript tradition. A researcher needs to have seen enough manuscripts to know what is common and what is extraordinary and what to expect from manuscripts originating from different places and periods. This kind of overview and insight rests only with a small number of experts.

BEFORE EMAILING

Before you email an expert, there are some things you should think through. If you know that you tend to ask for help too soon, then start by asking yourself whether you might find the answer to the inquiry yourself. To know the familiar insights and the frontiers of knowledge in a field, you have to read up, and you have to spend time with colleagues in that field, getting exposed over time to discussions and interactions. Becoming familiar with a field is the responsibility of all of us who do research. Remember, too, that an expert who has gained a reputation for being accessible may spend hours every day assisting others in their research. Also keep in mind that women academics are often perceived as more approachable and therefore end up doing more of this invisible work of answering questions from novices. You do not want to add to that workload unless there are good reasons to. In other words, make sure to do your homework.

On the other hand, if you are the type who asks for help only when it is almost too late, send that email along at once! You may be afraid of taking up someone else's time and adding to a workload that is already heavy. Sure, you will clutter the expert's inbox, but an expert in the field may be interested in what you are bringing to the table. You may also fear that your question is ignorant or trite. How do you know that it is legitimate? Very often, it is impossible for you to know. That is the nature of being a learner, whether you are a newly minted scholar or a more senior academic embarking on a new research project.

If you can check the following two boxes, chances are that your question is legitimate and that you should feel free to proceed.

☐ You have consulted the best reference tools and bibliographies available without finding the answer.
☐ You have read the CV of the expert you think you need to consult, and you have read everything the expert has written on the topic. (You want to avoid the response "Please see my 1998 publication on X.")

Contacting the expert may be intimidating. The risk of exposing ignorance evokes anxiety or shame in many of us. You may have been taught that doing research involves engaging in a kind of knowledge combat, and coming across as ignorant means that you are on the losing side. And yes, the academy can be competitive, but in many fields, you will find that your colleagues can be generous. When Brent looks back at some of his earliest emails to experts, he can see in retrospect both things he could—and should—have figured out on his own and just how gracious most of the experts were in leading him to the solutions to his problems in spite of his (painfully obvious) ignorance. True, some experts may regard research as a form of intellectual martial art. One thing is certain, however: if you choose not to contact an expert, you will not learn from the best.

COMPOSING THE MESSAGE

When you compose your message, be simple, polite, and precise. Keep it short. Briefly introduce yourself, ask focused questions, and always, always say "thank you." Your email may look like one of the samples in Box 7.1 or Box 7.2.

After you double-check it, push "Send." Then be patient.

It can be hard to be kept waiting and difficult to interpret a silence. The expert may have missed your email in a bursting inbox, may not want to engage with your question, or may be completely overwhelmed at the moment but will answer you next month or next season. Whatever the situation is, wait at least a couple of weeks before you send a very gentle reminder. See Box 7.3 for an example.

BOX 7.1. Sample Email to Expert 1

Dear Professor Ivy Tweed,

I hope this email finds you well.

My name is Liv Ingeborg Lied and I am a professor of the Study of Religion in Oslo. The two of us have unfortunately never met, but I am a great admirer of your work and I am aware of your publications on manuscript X.

I am currently working on this manuscript, and I have come across an annotation on folio 111r that I am unable to understand. The annotation reads ÆØÅ. I have not seen any similar annotations in other manuscripts that I have consulted, and it is not mentioned in the otherwise excellent handbook that you coedited with Professor Sophia Knowitall. Have you ever come across this annotation in your work?

I would be deeply grateful for any suggestions you might have and any insights you may be willing to share with me. Please, I do not want you to take on any additional work for my sake. If you do not know the answer from the top of your head, simply let me know, and I will continue my search.

Thank you so much in advance!

Kind regards,

Liv Ingeborg Lied

Acknowledgments and a Caveat

This morning, when you checked your email, the reply from the expert was waiting for you. If you receive a reply that communicates between the lines that the expert considers your

Asking for Help

153

BOX 7.2. Sample Email to Expert 2

Dear Professor Expert,

My name is Brent Nongbri, and I am a researcher working on early Christian manuscripts. I have learned a great deal from your expertise in bookbinding, and I wonder if I could prevail upon you to read and offer feedback on an essay that I have written on the basics of ancient book construction. I've relied on the work of Szirmai and other resources (including your own recent survey article). Nevertheless, I find myself still a little confused about the proper usage of bookbinding terms and the details of particular types of stitching. For example, is a whipstitch the same as overcasting, or are they two distinct techniques, or is a whipstitch a variety of stabbing? Questions about this kind of specialist terminology are hard for an outsider like me, especially when I see what appear to be conflicting usages in the literature.

If you're not able to read the essay at this time, please feel free to just say "No." I will completely understand.

Thanks very much for your time and trouble.

Best wishes,

Brent Nongbri

---

question to be banal, remember that it is better to lose face now, while you are still becoming familiar with manuscript study, than after you have published the outcome of your research. Or maybe the expert does not know the answer to your query and says so. Take that as a sign that you are indeed onto something interesting. Whether or not you get an answer that

BOX 7.3. Sample of a Gentle Reminder

Dear Professor Expert,

I don't wish to make a pest of myself, but I did want to check in to confirm that you received my earlier message regarding manuscript X.

I thank you again for your time and consideration.

All the best,

Brent Nongbri

---

solves your puzzle, make sure to send a gracious thank-you. If the information the expert shares with you becomes important to your research, always, *always* acknowledge the assistance in any publication.

We should not end this discussion without mentioning one further potential drawback to contacting an expert. Ideally, the person you contact will take an interest in your question and provide you with a helpful answer. But it is possible that someone could take *too much* interest in your question and perhaps respond in a way that suggests that your idea is actually his or hers. That could be the case. The expert may have published on this topic and may have a reference to provide you. But it may also be the case that the expert recognizes that you have a good idea but is the type of person who regularly assumes that he or she personally is the ultimate source of *all* good ideas, including yours. Such an assumption can place you in a very awkward situation. After all, you contacted the expert who has now taken ownership of your question. If something like this happens, talk to a trusted mentor and seek advice. You may have to make a judgment call. You could quickly try to attach your name to the idea in a public way, through social media or in a conference presentation. But doing so would be a bit of a tightrope walk; you do not want to appear to be taking the work of another without giving due credit. The situation would be very tricky. Hopefully it never arises for you.

Research in the 2020s is not a solitary endeavor. Despite the possible risks involved, there is much more to gain than to fear from interacting with your peers, being part of the ongoing discussion within an academic community, and reaching out to an expert.

Further Reading

Grafton, Anthony. *Worlds Made by Words: Scholarship and Community in the Modern West.* Cambridge, MA: Harvard University Press, 2011.

Nicholas, David, and Ian Rowlands. "Social Media Use in the Research Workflow." *Information Services and Use* 31, nos. 1–2 (2011): 51–83.

Soskice, Janet. *The Sisters of Sinai: How Two Lady Adventurers Discovered the Hidden Gospels.* New York: Vintage, 2010.

8

Publishing and Permissions

As you are analyzing the results of your research and organizing them, you are no doubt looking forward to publishing your findings. What steps do you need to take in order to use images of manuscripts in your publications? What about unpublished archival materials relating to questions of provenance?

In addition to all the usual protocols of academic publication, research involving manuscripts often entails reproducing images of manuscripts or reporting details about unpublished manuscripts or archival records. There are several practicalities to think about as you navigate these processes. Although more and more collections are implementing open access policies, many collections still require explicit permission to use images of manuscripts and archival material, and many still charge fees. Our goal in this chapter is to offer advice about obtaining permissions and to suggest some work-arounds for problems. Be aware that institutional guidelines are constantly changing. What we offer in this chapter is a summary of permissions practices as we have experienced them. Some issues in this chapter will intersect with copyright laws in different countries. We are not lawyers, so you may need to seek other resources if legal questions come up.

Requesting Permissions from Owning Institutions

For both images and unpublished texts, you want to be sure that you clearly understand the rights and permissions policies of owning institutions and rights holders. Although the people who produced ancient manuscripts are now long dead, and the anonymous character of most of the copyists prevents any identification of their descendants, the rules of copyright still, somewhat counterintuitively, apply to photos and drawings of ancient manuscripts. Publishing images thus requires obtaining permission from the library, museum, monastery, or other entity that owns the manuscript. On many occasions, the owners will also be the rights holders. But you may need to request permission from both a library (owning institution) and, for example, a photographer—specifically, the creator and holder of the rights for the media you will reproduce in your work.

Requesting permission can be a very simple process. You begin by checking the website of the owning institution. Most museums and libraries have established policies about the use of images, and they often have an online form requesting all the information they need in order to grant permission to publish an image of one or more of their manuscripts. Note that this process is distinct from purchasing the images themselves. The data requested for granting permissions may include, but is not limited to:

- your name and contact details
- the shelfmark (and, if relevant, folio number or numbers) of the item that you want to reproduce
- details about the publication in which the reproduction will appear, which can determine whether you need to pay fees (an academic journal? a book? something else?)

- the type of image (a full view of a page? a detailed view of a line or word?)
- the anticipated size of the reproduction (quarter page? half page? full page? double-page spread?)
- information about where the image will appear, which can also affect the fee (book jacket? journal interior?)
- the anticipated circulation of the journal or the print run of the book and maybe information about e-books and Internet subscriptions to journals (the publishers can provide this information)
- the anticipated price of the journal or book

Depending on the institution, securing permission can take some time. It is a good idea to get started as soon as you know where your research will be published. You may find yourself caught between, on the one hand, a publisher or journal that requires permissions to be in place before they will send your work out for review and, on the other hand, an owning institution that demands to know exactly where your work will be published before granting permission. In any case, securing permissions is a process, so be sure to allow plenty of time.

For a variety of reasons, your original plans to work with a particular academic journal or publisher could fall through. If you secure the rights for your images but then find that your work is not going to be published in the outlet that you originally named in your request, what can you do? In most cases, owning institutions will be flexible about publishing elsewhere as long as the kind of publication remains the same. If you change from one journal to another, most owning institutions will allow that shift. If, however, you switch from publishing the reproduction in an academic journal to publishing it in a book aimed at a popular audience, expect the owning institution to charge you an extra fee.

In the best-case scenario, institutions will have an open-access policy about the use of images of their manuscripts. Yet even if an institution does have such a policy, there may still be requirements connected to the use of the images. For instance, the Fondation Martin Bodmer in Geneva has an open-access policy for the large collection of online images of its manuscripts, but there are still some conditions of use. The site that hosts the images of the manuscripts carries the following statement: "Unless otherwise specified, the contents of this site are published under a Creative Commons CC-BY-NC, 4.0 license." Clicking on the CC link takes you to the relevant Creative Commons page that lists the conditions of use, which include proper source attribution. You can expect a similar request from all owning institutions, which may have very different preferred forms of credit.

Requests Using Publishers' Templates

When owning institutions do not have explicit policies, journals and publishers may have guidelines about the rights they expect you to acquire in order for them to publish the images. Publishers are usually very careful about copyrights and permissions because they want to avoid having any legal troubles with any rights holders who perceive improper use of materials for which they hold copyright. To avoid trouble, publishers have their own protocols in place to make sure that all necessary permissions for use of images or archival material are obtained. Presses often provide authors with templates for requesting images and the permission to use them. Such templates will likely make a broad request for use of the image, using language like "nonexclusive world rights in all formats and all languages." This means that the publisher is asking for the right to use the reproduction of the image of the manuscript in both the present edition and all later editions, whether print or electronic. Having these broad rights makes publishers' operations easier, but sometimes rights holders will not grant you all those reproduction rights. If you are not able to get such extensive rights, you can take a more limited set of rights to your publisher and see what the publisher can do. The bottom line is to make sure that you, the rights holder, and the publisher are all in agreement. Nobody wants to be surprised when it comes to rights and permissions.

When requesting rights, it can be a good idea to pose a question along these lines: "If you do not control the rights requested, I would be grateful to learn to whom I should apply." The party that you think is the rights holder may turn out not to be. This often happens if you are working with archival material relating to the provenance of your manuscript. The holding institution may have copies of letters that provide important information about the provenance of the manuscript, but the rights holder may be the estate of the author of the letters. In such cases, you need to seek out any potential rights holders. This process is called **due diligence**. Since it can be time consuming, begin the search as soon as you have a clear idea of where your work will be published. Keep records of all your correspondence related to the search, for your publisher will probably want to see evidence that you searched in the event that you are unable to locate a rights holder.

When Images or Permissions Aren't Forthcoming

Hopefully, your request for permission goes smoothly using the owning institution's forms. But there may be occasions when things don't quite go according to plan. For instance, an

Publishing and Permissions

institution may be unwilling or unable to provide images to you in a timely fashion. Sometimes manuscripts are undergoing an extended period of conservation. Sometimes they are traveling in exhibitions. And sometimes they are too fragile to be moved for photography. In such cases, you may need to find work-arounds. Sometimes owning institutions suggest alternatives, but sometimes you have to ask. If you are working with a large owning institution, you may need to shift your correspondence to a different department. The department of manuscripts may be the port of first call, but this department may direct you to the department of conservation or the archives, either of which might keep old photographs or negatives on hand. Ideally, all these departments have clear channels of communication, but you may need to navigate the different areas of the institution yourself.

Alternatively, you may need to seek out previously published images of your manuscript and try to use these in your own publication. As we suggested in Chapter 4, older images can be preferable if the manuscript you are studying has deteriorated or been damaged since the time of the earlier photography. This approach can, however, complicate the rights process, as most publishers will want both the owners and the earlier publishers to grant permission, but this strategy can be worth a try if you are in a pinch. Brent has successfully used it on several occasions. A similar approach involves seeking out previous owners of your manuscript, who also may have photos or negatives. Again, this would involve obtaining two sets of permissions.

There are also online sources of images, available either through payment or for free. Both options involve some risks. Paid image services like Getty Images are aimed more at commercial users and can be wildly expensive. Free options like Wikimedia Commons often rely on users who upload files but who have little or no knowledge of copyright law, so many files on these sites have incorrect copyright information and could leave you and your publisher liable to complaints from the actual copyright holders. It is always safest to begin your permissions queries with the owning institutions and to use third-party sources only as a last resort.

Other Scholars and "Your" Manuscript

In addition to considering the rights of the owning institution, you might look into the rights other scholars might have, or at least might perceive they have, to the study and publication of certain manuscripts. In the past, libraries and museums customarily granted the exclusive rights of publication or study of a manuscript to a particular scholar or team of scholars and allowed these people to maintain the rights for long periods of time. In such situations, scholars can feel that they own the manuscripts. This feeling can be natural and understandable. Throughout this book, we have used the phrase "your manuscript" to reflect the sense of closeness that comes with extended study of a manuscript. A scholar can spend a career working on a small set of manuscripts or even a single manuscript. At other times, however, this feeling of ownership can shade into a kind of pettiness or greed. In either case, it is important to ascertain whether another scholar claims ownership of the manuscript that you are studying. Reading widely in the most recent secondary literature and asking a curator can be good ways of finding out this information. If another scholar is working on the material, you can attempt to judge whether this person may be collaborative and helpful or competitive and protective. You may need to make a difficult judgment call about how to proceed.

Fortunately, this aspect of the field is rapidly changing. Curators and collections are much less likely now to make these kinds of agreements with scholars. If they do make such agreements, they are often for limited periods of time—say, three to five years instead of in perpetuity. And once again, digitization has changed the playing field by opening up the study of manuscripts, in a digitally mediated form, to a more globalized audience. This development makes it much harder to defend any exclusive claims to access or publication rights. So you may never encounter this kind of dilemma. Still, checking around is a good idea. You may even find a new colleague to consult.

Saving and Sharing Images

If you were able to take pictures or purchase bulk images of a manuscript, you may not publish all of the data that you collected. If you have concrete plans to publish the data in coming years, you may wish to maintain it privately. If you don't have plans to work with all the data you have collected, you may want to consider, in consultation with the owning institution, options for making your data more widely available. In fact, many state agencies that fund research now ask for you to have a specific management plan for the data generated by your research. If you do decide to keep the images private for any length of time, you may find yourself being approached by other scholars who ask to see the images. When you obtained the images, you may well have signed an agreement that forbids you to share the images, for the sale of photos and digital images is often a source of income for owning institutions. There is, however, a mostly unspoken agreement among many manuscript researchers that images of any kind can be shared for "research only" purposes. So again, you might need to make some tricky decisions about whom to trust.

Many of the challenges and pitfalls outlined in this chapter are rare occurrences. In most cases, the process of getting permissions is relatively smooth, if occasionally more drawn out and more expensive than it would be in an ideal world.

Further Reading

Association of University Presses website, https://aupresses
.org/permissions-faq/, for further information on the topic
of copyright and permissions.
Germano, William. *Getting It Published: A Guide for Scholars
and Anyone Else Serious about Serious Books.* 3rd ed.
Chicago: University of Chicago Press, 2016.

Conclusions

We hope this book has proven to be a useful guide as you take the first steps into the fascinating world of studying manuscripts. Ideally, having read these chapters, you are now in a position to approach manuscripts with greater confidence and with a broader set of questions. If you look back to the images of the codex containing the letters of Paul in the Introduction (see Figures I.1 and I.2), you might now see them from new angles. You will still be interested in learning what the main text inscribed on the pages says, but you might also ask what those other notes in the margin say. You might even ask the provenance question: How did these folia from a Greek manuscript end up in the Bibliothèque nationale in Paris? The Pinakes database would tell you that in fact parts of this same manuscript are also held in collections in Turin, Saint Petersburg (Russia), Moscow, Kyiv, and Mount Athos (Greece). Checking on the items in the bibliography in Pinakes would lead you back to Bernard de Montfaucon's catalog of the Coislin Library published in 1715. There you would learn that this codex of Paul's letters was taken apart at Mount Athos in the year 1218, and its folia were used as pastedowns in the manufacture of newer books at the monastery. This history explains both the oddly cut shapes of some of the folia (see Figure I.2 again) and the presence of pieces of the manuscript in so many different collections. How exactly these newer books made their way to their current locations is still being discovered.

If you determine that your research questions require you to see parts of this manuscript (or any manuscript) in person, the resources we have gathered here should assist you in arranging a successful visit, as well as in making effective use of the data that you collect. Hopefully, at the end of the process, you are able to produce an article, chapter, or book that incorporates your work with manuscripts in a satisfying way. Ideally, the overall experience should be academically fulfilling and—at a personal level—inspiring, stimulating, and fun.

Further Reading

Elia, Erika, and Rosa Maria Piccione. "A Rediscovered Library: Gabriel Severos and His Books." In *Greeks, Books, and Libraries in Renaissance Venice,* ed. Rosa Maria Piccione, 33–82. Berlin: De Gruyter, 2021.

Montfaucon, Bernard de. *Bibliotheca Coisliniana, olim Segueriana.* Paris: Ludovicus Guerin and Carolus Robustel, 1715.

Glossary

This glossary provides definitions for some terms used in the book that may be unfamiliar or that have special meanings when used in the context of the study of manuscripts.

Ancient Media Criticism: A research perspective that highlights the mediating functions and potential agency of media in the ancient communication cycle and in the "crafting of the message." Ancient media includes, for example, manuscripts and other products of literacy, as well as oral communications, performances, and collective memory.

apparatus: See **critical apparatus**.

bifolium (or bifolio, plural bifolia): A folded sheet forming two folia in a codex. Bifolia are stacked and folded to form a quire.

book block: The bound stack of quires that make a codex or, in the case of a single-quire codex, the single bound quire that constitutes the codex.

Book History: The historical study of books as material artifacts and of texts as recorded forms. Book Historians explore the historiography of the book: aspects relating to the production, dissemination, circulation, reception, and appropriation of books.

codex (plural codices): A book with pages (as opposed to a roll).

codicological unit: A discrete element in the structure of a codex; a quire or set of quires produced as part of a single act of production; sometimes called a production unit.

168   Glossary

codicology: The study of material and structural features of codices.

colophon: A formulaic note from the copyist of a manuscript to readers.

composite codex: A codex composed of codicological units (quires or booklets) issued during distinct phases of production.

copy: A unique instance of a text as it occurs in a manuscript ("That roll contains a copy of Genesis"), but sometimes a synonym for "manuscript" ("That roll is a copy of Genesis").

copyist: The person(s) responsible for writing the text of a manuscript.

critical apparatus: In critical editions, the system used to present variant readings preserved in manuscript copies of a text but rejected by the editors of the critical edition. The critical apparatus usually occupies the lower part of the page in a critical edition, below the text reconstructed by the editors.

critical edition: A printed edition of a textual work that is assembled by scholars who apply rules of textual criticism to produce a single stable text out of the multiple different texts transmitted in the surviving manuscripts of the text. This critical text is accompanied by an apparatus at the bottom of the page showing the (rejected) variant or alternative readings preserved in the manuscripts.

cursive: Writing that takes place with few instances of the stylus or pen being lifted off the page. Cursive writing is characterized by letters connected to one another.

delimitation markers: Symbolic marks that communicate the beginning, the end, or a pause in a sense unit or a reading unit.

doodles: Scribbles and rough drawings.

DPI: "dots per inch." DPI indicates image quality / resolution: the higher the DPI, the sharper the image.

due diligence: In the context of publishing copyrighted material, the process of making every reasonable effort to find a rights holder and secure permission from the rights holder for use of the copyrighted material.

eisthesis: The indentation of the beginning of a line of text (the opposite of ekthesis); often used to indicate a sense break or a new section.

Glossary

ekthesis: The projection of the beginning of a line of text beyond the limit of the written column (the opposite of indentation); often used to indicate a sense break or a new section. Also spelled ecthesis.

endbands: Bands at the head and tail of the spine edge of a book block attached by stitching through the centers of the quires.

exemplar: The manuscript that serves as the model for a copyist who is producing a new manuscript.

explicit: The ending of a text, sometimes marked by increased letter size, inks in contrasting colors, or decoration; from the Latin *explicare,* "to unroll," since end titles for books were customarily found at the end, or innermost portion, of a roll.

flyleaf: A folium at the end or beginning of the book block, located between the binding and the book block.

foliation: The numbering of the folia of a codex, with the numbers usually placed on the recto in the upper margin.

folium (or folio, plural folia): A leaf of a codex (one half of a bifolium); sometimes abbreviated as fol. or f.

fore edge: The side of the book block opposite the spine.

frons **(plural** *frontes***)**: The top or bottom of a closed papyrus roll.

gathering: See **quire**.

Gregory's Rule: In the formation of quires, the pattern of bifolium placement that results in "like facing like"—that is, in parchment codices, hair side faces hair side and flesh side faces flesh side, and in papyrus codices, horizontal fibers face horizontal fibers and vertical fibers face vertical fibers.

gutter: The inner margin of a codex page; the area near the fold or spine.

head: The top of a codex or book block.

incipit: The opening word or words of a text, sometimes marked by increased letter size, inks in contrasting colors, or decoration.

intercolumn (or intercolumnar space): The (originally) uninscribed area between two columns.

kollēma **(plural** *kollēmata***)**: A sheet of papyrus.

kollēsis **(plural** *kollēseis***)**: The area of overlap resulting from two papyrus *kollēmata* being pasted together to form a roll.

lacuna (plural lacunae): A gap in the text on a manuscript caused by damage, erasure, or defacing.

lamella (plural lamellae): Flattened metal sheets, often lead or gold, inscribed with text.

layout: the appearance of a written page (placement of columns of writing, size of margins, etc.), sometimes referred to using the French phrase *mise en page* (literally, the "putting-on-the-page").

leaf: see **folium**.

maceration: The step in the process of making paper in which plant material is soaked and broken up in order to free cellulose fibers to mix into the water.

majuscule: Writing characterized by the use of capital letters, which are generally unconnected to one another (as opposed to minuscule script).

manuscript: An inscribed object containing, among other things, text written by hand; sometimes abbreviated as ms (plural mss).

margins: The areas of a page that surround the text block.

marginalia: Annotations inscribed on the margins of a page.

Material Philology (sometimes called New Philology): A branch of editorial theory and a perspective on textual scholarship that advocates the exploration of texts as they occur in the manuscripts that embody them. Material Philologists highlight the textual and material individualities of each copy of a text and view the material embodiment as part of the constitution of the text.

metadata: Data about data; in the context of digital images, data about the image (date, time, and place the image was made; description of the image; make of the camera that captured the image; lighting conditions, etc.).

minuscule: A neat, formalized type of cursive script (as opposed to majuscule script).

miscellaneous codex: A codex containing texts that form no obvious corpus. Miscellaneous codices may contain texts of several genres or combine texts from several corpora.

Glossary   171

mise en page: See **layout.**

opening: The open codex showing two pages (a verso and a recto).

opisthograph: A roll that has been inscribed with a continuous text on both its inner and its outer surfaces.

ostracon (plural ostraca): A potsherd or similarly sized flat stone incised with writing or inscribed with ink.

page: One of the two faces of a folium or leaf.

paleography (or palaeography): The study of the writing on manuscripts. In the nineteenth century, the word "paleography" referred to the study of ancient and medieval manuscripts more broadly, encompassing not only the study of the development of scripts but also what is now usually called "codicology."

palimpsest: A manuscript that has been erased and reused to copy a new text. A palimpsest contains a (partly) visible erased layer of writing under a later inscribed layer (or layers) of writing.

pandect: In the context of Christian manuscripts, a codex that contains a (perceived) complete Bible; in a Roman legal context, a compendium of fifty books containing excerpts of the writings of Roman jurists.

paper: Writing surface produced from plant-based pulp that is pressed and dried.

papyrology: Literally, the study of papyrus manuscripts but broadly a field which in practice encompasses the editing and study of many different inscribed media, including papyrus, parchment, leather, and ostraca.

papyrus (plural papyri): Writing surface produced from flattened strips of the pith of the reeds of the *Cyperus papyrus* plant.

paratext: In manuscript scholarship, a diverse array of verbal and nonverbal content (text, images, diagrams) that facilitate communication between the work copied on a manuscript's page and its producers, on the one hand, and its real or presumed readers, on the other. Paratexts share the page with the main text (the text copied in the columns), appear alongside the text, and communicate beyond the text, but are relevant primarily owing to their relationship to the text; titles and annotations are examples of paratexts.

parchment: Writing surface produced from processed animal hides dried under tension.

pastedown: A folium that is pasted to the inside of a cover.

prickings: Small holes puncturing a writing surface to establish the limits of the text block.

prōtokollon: The first sheet (*kollēma*) of a roll, often left blank to serve as protection for the inscribed inner sheets of the roll.

provenance: A record or narrative of the history of an artifact's movement and claimed ownership.

provenience: The point of origin of an object. The term can refer to the place of production, or in the case of an excavated artifact, the place of excavation or discovery.

quire (or gathering or signature): A stack of folded sheets (bifolia) used to form a book block.

quire signature: Number written in the margin of the first or last page (or first *and* last page) of a quire indicating the quire's position in the book block.

recto: In codicological terms, the face of the folium that comes first in reading order—thus, the right-hand page of an opening for codices with texts in Greek, Latin, and other languages that are read left to right, and the left-hand page of an opening for Syriac, Arabic, and other languages read right to left. In reference to rolls, "recto" is sometimes used to indicate the front, or first inscribed side, of the roll. For papyrus rolls, this is usually the side on which the writing runs parallel to the fibers.

roll: A book or document written, usually in multiple columns, on a continuous surface made of one or more sheets and closed by rolling up.

rubrication: the use of colored ink (usually red)—as opposed to the black ink most commonly used in manuscripts—to highlight certain portions of text. The term is derived from the Latin *ruber,* "red."

ruling: Written or incised guidelines on a page to help copyists produce neat lines (horizontal ruling) and to keep the inscribed text within the limits of the column layout (vertical ruling).

Glossary

scholion (plural scholia): In Greek and Latin manuscripts, a scholarly annotation on a passage; sometimes used in a more general sense for any marginal note containing commentary or explanatory information.

sense line: A type of sense unit created by copying a text in lines corresponding to a grammatical unit (a phrase or sentence), as opposed to copying a text in a continuous script.

sense unit: A grammatically coherent portion of text identified by some graphic feature of a manuscript (for example, special spacing or punctuation); sometimes called a sense division.

shelfmark: A unique identifier used by the holding institution to sort its manuscript materials.

siglum (plural sigma): A letter, number, or combination of letters and numbers that refers to a manuscript. Sigla are often used in the apparatuses of critical editions in order to save space.

sizing: The application of starch, gelatin, or other materials to paper to make its surface less porous and thus less likely to allow ink to bleed.

snake weight: Beaded weights (usually covered in fabric) used to safely hold a codex open.

spine: The bound side of the book block.

superscript title: A title that appears in the margin above and at a certain distance from the text in the text block, visually semi-detached from that text by means of, for instance, the script size and skipped line space in addition to the color of the ink.

tacket: A cord composed of thread or twisted leather or parchment passed through holes in the central fold of a quire and tied in a loop in order to secure the bifolia of the quire or to attach the quire to a cover.

tail: The bottom of a codex or book block.

text block: The written area of a page, sometimes defined by ruling; also sometimes a reference to what is more properly called the book block.

textual scholar: A scholar trained in the interpretation of texts, though not necessarily in the study of the manuscripts that carry texts.

title: A phrase that formulates an established identification of a literary entity; when present, the title is most commonly graphically distinguished from the rest of the text copied on the page by, for example, the color of the ink, spacing, the size of the letters, or the use of decoration.

union catalog: A catalog that includes data about the holdings of several different library collections.

vellum: Generally used as a synonym for "parchment" but sometimes used more specifically to refer to calfskin prepared as a writing surface.

verso: In codicological terms, the face of the folium that comes second in reading order—thus, the left-hand page of an opening for codices with texts in Greek, Latin, and other languages that read left to right, and the right-hand page of an opening for Hebrew, Arabic, and other languages read right to left. In reference to rolls, "verso" is sometimes used to indicate the back side of the roll, whether blank or secondarily inscribed (for papyrus rolls, this is usually, though not always, the side on which the writing runs against the fibers).

Notes

2. Finding Your Manuscript

1. James Robinson, *The Manichean Codices of Medinet Madi* (Cambridge, UK: James Clark & Co, 2015), 156.

3. Provenance and Why It Matters

1. Society for Classical Studies, "SCS Statement on Professional Ethics," revised 2023, https://classicalstudies.org/about/scs-statement-professional -ethics.

2. James Cuno, *Who Owns Antiquity? Museums and the Battle over Our Cultural Heritage* (Princeton: Princeton University Press, 2008), xxxvi.

3. Monica Hanna, "Cultural Heritage Attrition in Egypt," in *Testing the Canon of Ancient Near Eastern Art and Archaeology,* ed. Amy Rebecca Gansell and Ann Shafer (Oxford: Oxford University Press, 2020), 315.

4. Patty Gerstenblith, "Hobby Lobby, the Museum of the Bible, and the Law," in *Antiquities Smuggling in the Real and Virtual World,* ed. Layla Hashemi and Louise Shelley (New York: Routledge, 2022), 59–95, at 84.

5. John Boardman, "Archaeologists, Collectors, and Museums," in *Whose Culture? The Promise of Museums and the Debate over Antiquities,* ed. James Cuno (Princeton: Princeton University Press, 2012), 117–118.

6. Akinwumi Ogundiran, "The License of Power in African Art," *African Arts* 53 (2020): 18–19, at 19.

5. In the Reading Room with Your Manuscript

1. Nestle-Aland, 28th edition: Institute for New Testament Textual Research Münster/Westphalia, ed., *Novum Testamentum Graece*, 28th rev. ed. (Stuttgart: Deutsche Bibelgesellschaft, 2012).

6. Back Home—What Now?

1. Henry A. Sanders, *Facsimile of the Washington Manuscript of the Minor Prophets in the Freer Collection and the Berlin Fragment of Genesis* (Ann Arbor: University of Michigan, 1927), ix.

Index

abbreviations, 30–31, 43–44, 49, 59
access. *See* repositories and
collections
Ancient Media Criticism, 6, 167
Apocrypha, 48–49, 147
apparatus. *See* critical apparatus
archival research, 58–59, 82,
133–135
auction houses, 45, 57, 82–83

binding, 123. *See also* covers
Book History, 6, 10, 167
budgeting. *See under* travel

Codex Coislinianus (Paris, Bibliothèque nationale de France,
Coislin 202), 2–5, 165–166
Codex Vaticanus (Vatican City,
Biblioteca Apostolica Vaticana,
Gr. 1209), 120–121
codices: diagrams of, 20, 22–23;
distinguished from rolls, 19,
126–128; parts of, 19–26; scholarship on, 39–40
codicological units, 42, 124–125, 167
colonialism, 7–8, 64–66, 78–80, 87
colophons: examples of, 2–4, 30–32;
purposes of, 119, 121, 123–124, 168
composite codices, 124–125, 168

conservation of manuscripts:
alerting staff to the need for,
113, 131; decay and, 36; effect on
access, 97; scholarship on, 40
copyright. *See* permissions
corrections, 32, 34, 117, 119–121
covers, 17–18, 23–25. *See also* binding
critical apparatus: definition, 168;
limits of, 122; use of, 2, 47, 116,
128–129
critical editions: definition, 1–2,
168; familiar aspects of, 6,
100; use of, 2, 47, 116, 121–122,
128–129
cultural heritage: conceptual
debates concerning, 72–74, 86;
damage to or destruction of, 57,
69; laws regarding, 68–70, 84

Dead Sea Scrolls, 56–57, 59, 113, 115
digital images: access to, 6, 163;
benefits and drawbacks of, 90,
92–93, 106, 141; manipulation of,
34, 130, 141; online collections of,
91; organization of, 132, 136–139;
sharing, 163; taking your own,
103, 123, 132. *See also* photographs; Wikimedia Commons
divination, 10

178 Index

drawings, 30, 32
due diligence, 71, 74, 160, 168

ekthesis, 28, 130, 169
erasure, 16, 32–34, 117–118, 121
ethics. *See* legal and ethical
guidelines

finding aids for manuscripts,
45–46, 59–62
foliation, 28, 30, 169
forgeries, 67
fragments, 51, 56, 113, 126–131

gatherings. *See* quires
Getty Images, 161
gloves, 113–114
Gregory's Rule, 19, 169

Hague Convention (1954), 69
handwriting. *See* paleography
help, asking an expert for, 149–155.
See also social media
heritage. *See* cultural heritage

images. *See* digital images;
photographs
ink, 5, 15–16, 38, 130–131

laws. *See* legal and ethical
guidelines
layout: definition and general
discussion of, 26–28, 170; effects
on interpretation of text, 4–5,
124–125; scholarship on, 40
legal and ethical guidelines:
academic bodies and, 70–72, 83,
87–88; international agreements,
68–70; running afoul of, 84
London, British Library, Add.
14,687, 33–35
looting, 68

manuscript hunters, 65, 79–80,
96–97
Manuscript Studies: as distinct
from the topic of this book, 6;
elitism of, 92, 101; expert
knowledge and, 144; introductions to, 37; travel and, 89, 100
manuscripts: aspects to observe,
114–116; differences from printed
texts, 11; finding aids for, 45–46,
59–62; loss or destruction of,
57–59; materials of production,
14–16, 38–39; monetary value of,
42, 67; movement of, 42; naming
conventions for, 43, 51, 59 (*see
also* abbreviations); splitting
and combining of, 42; traces of
handling, 5, 10, 29–36, 40.
See also conservation of
manuscripts
marginal notation, 5, 30, 120–121
margins, 22–23, 27, 170
Material Philology, 6, 10, 37–38, 170
metadata, 123, 137–139, 143, 170
miscellaneous codices, 44, 124, 170
mise en page. *See* layout
models, 25
monasteries, 74–75, 79–80, 96–98

New Testament manuscripts, 2–5,
48, 128–129
note taking. *See* recordkeeping

opisthographs, 18–19, 127, 171
Oxyrhynchus papyri, 49–52, 57,
128–131

page numbers, 28, 126
paleography, 11–14, 118–119, 171
palimpsests, 16, 171
paper, 15–16
papyrus, 14–15

Index

papyrus roll. *See under* rolls
paratext, 27, 171
parchment, 15
Paris, Bibliothèque nationale de
France, Coislin 202, 2–5, 165–166
Paris, Bibliothèque nationale de
France, lat. 9561, 30–31
permissions, 156–162
Peshitta, 52–55, 59
photographs, 58–59, 141, 157, 161.
See also digital images
printing, 11–12
privilege, 77, 85, 98, 102
provenance: colonialism and,
64–66; definition, 63, 172;
questions to ask yourself
concerning, 81; strategies for
determining, 81–83. *See also*
legal and ethical guidelines;
provenience
provenience, 63–64, 172. *See also*
provenance

quire signatures, 28
quires, 19–21, 25, 28, 172

reading rooms: appropriate attire
for, 103–104; equipment in,
111–113; first visit to, 108–110;
potentially strange opening
hours of, 100; as social spaces,
134–135
recordkeeping, 131–133, 136–143
repositories and collections:
accessing, 94–98, 106–107;

histories of, 86–87; planning a
visit to, 98–105; typology of,
74–75
reuse, 18–19, 23–25, 32–35, 127
rolls: diagram of, 18; distinguished
from codices, 19, 126–128;
papyrus, 17–19; parchment,
17–18; scholarship on, 39
ruling, 17, 172

scroll. *See* rolls
sense line, 4, 173
sense unit, 4, 28, 173
Septuagint manuscripts, 47
social media, 144–149, 155
St. Catherine's Monastery Arabic
Manuscript 289, 32–33

textual scholar, 1–2, 9–10, 173
textual variants, 116–122
titles, 27, 29, 123–125, 173–174
travel: accommodations during,
101–102; budgeting for, 99–100;
necessity of, 90, 92; what to
bring, 102–105

UNESCO, 69–70, 72–73, 77
union catalog, 42, 174

Vatican City, Biblioteca Apostolica Vaticana, Gr. 1209,
120–121
vellum, 15, 174

Wikimedia Commons, 161–162